SHAKESPEARE QUESTIONS

AN OUTLINE FOR THE STUDY
OF THE LEADING PLAYS

BY

ODELL SHEPARD 1884-

16-12267

HOUGHTON MIFFLIN COMPANY

BOSTON · NEW YORK · CHICAGO · DALLAS

SAN FRANCISCO

The Riverside Press Cambridge

The Riverside Press
CAMBRIDGE . MASSACHUSETTS
PRINTED IN THE U. S. A

TO
PAUL SPENCER WOOD

CONTENTS

SHAKESPEARE QUESTIONS

INTRODUCTION

IT would be easy to expect more from this book than it is designed to give. It offers little criticism or information and it is not intended for use to the exclusion of lectures, books of reference, or notes. Indeed, it avoids, in as far as possible, the material commonly found in these indispensable helps and guides to the study of Shakespeare. It cannot take the place of a gifted interpreter nor can it make the men and women of the plays live and move before an inert mind or a listless imagination. It is primarily analytical in method, and although much has been done in the general questions to insure a comprehensive view of each play, the work of final synthesis has been left, as it always must be left, to the individual student.

I am aware of many objections that may be urged against a book such as the present, but I have yet to discover any method of teaching and studying Shakespeare as effective as the one upon which the book is based. The pure lecture system leaves the student too much upon his own resources and gives that impression of haziness and generality which leads to frequent and legitimate complaints against some methods of teaching English literature. The use of wide collateral reading is essential to the success of any method, but every teacher of the plays knows the danger of losing sight of Shakespeare while threading the jungle of Shakespearean scholarship. Reliance upon notes, dissection of the plays line by line and word by word " in disconnection dead and spiritless," use of the text as an exercise-book in etymology, phonetics, antiquities, and prosody, is probably the worst method of all. In this outline I have tried to steer a middle course between the Scylla of æstheticism and the Charybdis of pedantry — with the result, quite possibly, of

splintering my keel upon both. I have kept one mark, however, pretty steadily in view. I have asked myself repeatedly : Would Shakespeare himself be interested in this
question? Did he give this matter any thought, or should
he have done so? I hope I have asked few questions to
which the poet could not have given an intelligible answer.

This book represents an attempt to correct the American
student's aversion to hard, independent thinking on literary
matters — an aversion which has been fostered, at least, by
the multiplication of annotated editions and critical supple-
ments, and by the pure lecture method. After using this
outline of study for several years in college classes and
Shakespeare clubs, I feel justified in saying that it gives
definition, purpose, and direction to a subject which, in my
own teaching at least, is too likely to vanish into the thin air
of abstract theorizing or to die out in the thirsty sands of
mere fact-peddling. The outline insures at least two read-
ings of each play. It fixes the student's attention upon matters of real importance. It forces him to go back and back
to the text, not to an encyclopædia, until he is thoroughly
familiar with each play in its general aspects and in its more
important details. It provides numerous cross-references
from act to act and from play to play which are intended to
acquaint the learner with Shakespeare's whole work, to give
him some notions of the growth of the poet's mind and art,
and, incidentally, to show that we often need not only an
act or a play, but an epoch, in order to explain a single
word. The outline makes the student's work and results
more definite and tangible than they often are, and yet, unless I have failed completely in my purpose, it leaves the
play a living thing. Most important of all, the student is
constituted his own critic, though he is still under guidance.
He is asked at every turn, not to record the opinion of some
other student of the play or the conflicting opinions of a
score of others, but to base an intelligent, defensible opinion
of his own upon the evidence he can gather from the text.
Other methods give other results, but this seems to me the
only method for the beginner as it should be the chief method
used by the finished Shakespearean scholar.

A few words should be said about the use of the book in the classroom. It is the writer's custom to insist that all answers be written out so that they may be read from the notebook in recitation and to refuse to give credit for any answer not so given. This eliminates all stammering, extemporaneous replies and renders the answers more direct and specific than they could otherwise be. Necessarily, the questions are of widely varying difficulty. While they are not, for the most part, too difficult for students of high-school age, they have been used successfully with graduate students. They should be selected and graded by the instructor to suit the needs and maturity of his class. I have marked with an asterisk those questions which, because of their difficulty or because of the time they demand, should be assigned to individual students for special study and report. It may be found advantageous to assign others in this way. There are some questions, and those not the least valuable, which cannot be definitely and finally answered, but the value of class discussion of such moot points is obvious. The general questions should be considered in full before the set of detailed questions is taken up and a short interval should then be allowed for the second reading of the play.

The line-numbering used in this book is that of the *Globe* edition. It is employed in the *Temple*, the *Tudor*, and the *Arden* editions and in the editions of Neilson and Herford. It is recorded on each page of the *First Folio* edition, and is recognized as standard in modern books of reference. Professor W. A. Neilson's *Cambridge Poets* edition, which provides an excellent text of extraordinary accuracy together with compact but sufficient introductions, is the one which I have used in preparing this outline as well as in the classroom. There is an obvious advantage in the use of a single volume containing the poet's entire work.

My choice of the plays which I have treated has been determined by the needs of the average classroom and by the necessity that the book be kept as brief as possible.

For reasons of space, I have omitted all discussion of Shakespeare's dealing with source material. This omission would be a very grave one if it were not so easily repaired. By careful study of the sources of *As You Like It*, *Henry IV*, and *Othello*, or of any comedy, chronicle, and tragedy, the needs of all but the most advanced students should be met. I have purposely avoided frequent appeal to books of reference, criticism, and antiquities because I have wished to send the student constantly to the text as the last and best authority. A small number of books, of course, is indispensable, even for the beginner.

Any one who has penetrated even a little way into the thicket of Shakespearean scholarship finds his indebtedness too complex to record. I have compiled these questions with few books immediately at hand, thinking it best to subject myself to the same reliance upon the text which I have been engaged in recommending to others. I am especially indebted, however, to Professor A. H. Tolman's *Questions on Shakespeare* for the idea of including both general and detailed questions as well as for several hints as to the best use of such an outline as this in the classroom. It will be seen, however, that the scope and purpose of the present book are very different from those of Professor Tolman's work, which is in several volumes and includes a large body of critical and textual apparatus.

ODELL SHEPARD.

March 4, 1916.

A MIDSUMMER NIGHT'S DREAM

GENERAL QUESTIONS

1. Enumerate the actions or stories of the play. Which is the main and which the enveloping action? State the artistic purpose of this enveloping action. Compare, for effectiveness and harmony of tone, the enveloping action of *A Comedy of Errors*. Outline the method of passage from the real to the dream world in Act I.

2. Are the several actions harmonious one with another? What action is used for purposes of contrast? Name two distinct dramatic functions of the Bottom group.

3. Do you agree with Dowden's opinion that Theseus is the central figure of the play and the spring of its action? If not, who is?

4. At what time of the year does the action take place? What amount of time is indicated for the action in the first speeches of Act I? Is this the amount of time that actually does elapse? Try to explain discrepancies.

5. What evidences of immaturity do you find? What evidences of mature and masterly workmanship? Explain fully. Did rhymed lines and stichomythia increase or decrease with the poet's development? Point out and comment upon several cases of artificial, mechanical balance between characters and between actions. What effect did the poet try to secure by this artificial balance? What takes its place in his mature work?

6. What different kinds of verse are employed? For what special purposes and effects is each kind used? Does the verse form seem wisely chosen in all cases? For what effects does the poet use prose? Do you note any variation from the normal iambic beat of the verse? When is it used? Compare the Weird Sisters scenes in *Macbeth* and many of the songs and charms in *The Tempest*.

*7. In what way does this play show a marked technical and artistic advance upon the three earlier comedies? What general features has it in common with any or all of these? In what ways does it resemble opera and the Elizabethan masque? *

*8. This play created a new fairy world — the one with which we are now most familiar. How does its treatment of fairy life differ from that which preceded, as preserved in Milton's *L'Allegro*? Select five passages of special poetic magic and charm. Be prepared to explain your choice.

DETAILED QUESTIONS

I, 1.

1. What two actions are introduced and how are they welded together?
2. Point out at least one case of anachronism.
3. Are the motives governing the action of this scene always clear and convincing?

I, 2.

1. What preparation has been made for the action of this scene?
*2. Are the members of the Bottom group Athenian in character and manner? Is this a fault? Discuss fully. Mention other plays with foreign setting in which the same thing is seen. Would these fellows seem strange or familiar to Shakespeare's London audience? How would their presence affect that audience's acceptance of the play's legendary and supernatural elements?
3. Define and distinguish the characters of the men in the Bottom group.
4. Show that the poet has in mind local London stage conditions in this scene.

---

* Asterisks indicate questions which, in the author's opinion, are of sufficient difficulty to warrant their assignment to individual students for special research and report. Other questions should, in general, be prepared by the entire class.

*5. Classify Bottom's blunders in speech. Compare them with those of Launce in *Two Gentlemen of Verona*, with those of the Nurse in *Romeo and Juliet*, with those of Mistress Quickly in *II Henry IV* and those of Dogberry in *Much Ado*. Do you find that these five characters make errors of the same general sort? Where did the poet acquire his erudition in this field? Is it displayed appropriately in a play dealing with legendary Athens?

6. Compare all the remarks about the moon in this act. Comment.

II, 1.

1. How is the new action here introduced related to what precedes?

2. Why is this scene placed immediately after that dealing with the Bottom group?

3. How are the affairs of Oberon's court related to those of the human characters?

4. Define the character and functions of Puck. What preparation for later events is made in his boasting? Does Puck seem like the other fairies in all things?

*5. Study carefully the notes in the Furness Variorum edition upon 88–117 and 148–169. Make a defensible theory of your own on each of the problems involved.

6. Criticize the character of Helena as developed late in the scene. What excuse can you find for her?

II, 2.

1. Does this scene seem artificial and stiff or easy and natural? What elements contribute to this effect?

III, 1.

1. Does the actual prologue, as given in V, 1, correspond to that here planned?

2. What is the point of l. 26?

3. What is the second of the "hard things" referred to in 48–49? Compare the speaker with the other members of the group for ability and power of connected thought.

4. Make suggestions for the acting of this scene up to l. 78.

5. In what spirit are 145–150 spoken? Might any other member of the group have been chosen as appropriately as Bottom for the object of the enchantment and the love of Titania? Why?

6. Point out some of the incongruities of the situation presented in 167–206. By what means are they softened and beautified?

III, 2.

*1. Cite from other Shakespearean plays friendships between girls similar to that shown in 198–214. Why did the poet use such pairs of characters, especially of girls, so frequently? How and why used here? Contrast Hermia and Helena.

2. Would it be fair to draw any general inference from the fact that the girls are constant in their love from first to last, while the men change?

3. Outline the shifts in your sympathy for the various characters as the scene proceeds.

4. Make suggestions for the acting of Hermia's part in 191–277. Follow closely the movement of her thought. In what ways is the part of Lysander overdrawn? Compare l. 190.

5. Criticize the description of the dawn, 391–393.

6. How does the Lysander-Hermia-Demetrius-Helena action compare in interest with the other actions of the play? Give reasons. Do you grow fond of any of these? Do they seem real? How would the play have suffered if they had not been included?

IV, 1.

1. What evidence that Bottom does not remember the fairies' names or is otherwise forgetful?

2. In what ways is the delicacy of the fairies emphasized in 1–48?

3. Why does Titania surrender the changeling child so easily?

4. In what mood are 123–130 spoken? Were these words written, apparently, by a bookish, secluded poet, or by an

expert in huntsmanship and a lover of sports? Do they seem to have been written languidly or *con amore*? Compare *Venus and Adonis*, 673–708.

5. With 191–193 compare *Tempest*, IV, 1, 148–158. What gain in breadth and intensity of expression do you notice?

IV, 2.

1. Dramatic purpose and utility of this scene?
2. Discuss Bottom's manner upon his reappearance. What opinion of Bottom is held by his associates? Account for it. How does this opinion help to class and characterize those who hold it?

V, 1.

1. How many of the complications of the plot have been resolved before this scene opens? Is this a fault in structure? What necessary and important action is reserved for this act?
2. How much of Theseus' speech, 2–22, represents the poet's own belief? What, if anything, does it indicate regarding the poet's attitude toward the supernatural? Toward the poetic faculty? Do you wholly agree with those critics who say that Shakespeare makes Theseus praise the poet, in spite of Theseus' evident intention of doing just the contrary? Do not overlook the probably unconscious irony involved in making Theseus skeptical about poetry while he himself is dependent for his very existence upon the " shaping fantasies " of poets ancient and modern. So might Ajax or Hector speak, of whom, without Homer, we should never have heard.
3. Memorize 12–17.
4. Note the superior and high-handed way in which Theseus rejects or accepts the entertainment offered him. He is the " tired business man " of mythology. Remember that Shakespeare's livelihood largely depended upon his success in catering to a public and to individuals quite as capricious, preoccupied and superior as this Theseus. In what mood did the poet write these lines?

5. What determines Theseus' choice of the Pyramus and Thisbe play?

6. How do 89-105 support the interesting theory that this play was written for performance upon some state occasion and that the Bottom scenes were intended partly as a covert apology for the inadequate equipment at the poet's and the stage manager's command? Discuss the merits of this theory.

7. Punctuate Quince's prologue so as to make the sense he intended.

RICHARD II

GENERAL QUESTIONS

*1. Does this play belong to the rambling, epic type of chronicle play well represented in the three parts of *Henry VI*, or to the concentrated, unified type represented in Marlowe's *Edward II* and in Shakespeare's *Richard III?* See F. E. Schelling's *The English Chronicle Play* on Marlowe's *Edward II*.

*2. In what ways, if any, has the poet modified history with a view to concentrating or unifying his material? In what respects is the action incomplete? In what ways does the play fail of unity? Where has the dramatist brought historical events closer together than they were in reality? Why has he done so? What space of historical time does the action represent? In representing only this small portion of Richard's reign, does the play give a fair impression of the king's character and rule? See Green's *Short History of the English People,* chapter v, section 5, last three pages.

*3. Estimate the influence of Marlowe's *Edward II* upon this play in the following particulars: concentration of plot; suppression of comic relief; delineation of character; centralizing action about a single outstanding character or protagonist; treatment of royal favorites; versification. Is Marlowe's influence greater or less here than in *Richard III?* In what ways does the poet better his instruction? What features of the play make it clear that he is shaking off the influence of Marlowe?

*4. What is the central figure and spring of action? Show this in detail. Is our interest held primarily by the fall of Richard or by the rise of Bolingbroke? Is our attention held consistently to the central figure or is it dispersed over several persons? Compare *Richard III* in this respect. Compare the Henry VI and the Henry IV plays in this respect.

5. Has the action a well-marked initial incident, climax, and catastrophe? That is, has the poet tried to shape his material into the general form of tragedy? Do you think the initial action was well chosen as the germ of the action of the entire play?

6. Make a careful estimate of the character of Richard.

7. Make a careful estimate of the character of Bolingbroke.

8. Make a careful estimate of the character of York.

9. Do you discover growth in any or all of these characters or only a confirmation and intensification of qualities well developed from the start?

10. For what purpose were the figures of the three women introduced? Do the women act independently? Do they hinder action? Are they interesting in and for themselves? Do they illumine the characters of other persons in the play?

DETAILED QUESTIONS

I, 1.

1. Characterize the speeches of Mowbray and Bolingbroke. Which seems the more sincere? Which has the greater personal power? Can both be in the right?

2. What is the effect of Mowbray's hesitancy in speaking his mind about the king's cousin in the king's presence?

3. For what reasons does Richard wish to effect a reconciliation? How deep are those reasons? Do they do him credit? Comment especially upon 152–159.

4. With whom does the poet wish us to sympathize — the peace-making king or the blustering nobles? Having commanded peace, why does not Richard enforce it? How does he attempt to hide his defeat in 196–205?

5. Effect of the entire scene? Comment upon the large amount of rhyme. Why does the scene act better than it reads? Is it intended primarily for exposition or for some other purpose? What exposition does it contain? Is it a good first scene?

I, 2.

1. Comment upon the parallel similes of 11–21. Is this poetry or bad rhetoric?
2. With 37–41 compare III, 2, 56–57.
3. What do we learn of the characters of the two speakers in this scene? What exposition do you find? Is it cleverly interwoven with the speeches?

I, 3.

1. Is the predominating effect of 1–118 lyric, dramatic, or spectacular?
2. What is Richard's purpose in allowing the preliminaries for the duel to proceed so far? What effect does he intend that his action shall have? What effect does it have?
3. Are both Bolingbroke and Mowbray sincere in accepting the banishment?
4. What evidence do you find that Richard enjoys the part he is playing? Compare 148–153. What, especially, is the effect of the alliteration in 150–151? What does it indicate regarding the speaker's mood?
5. What great, new-found pride of Elizabethan England is indicated in 159–173?
6. How do 178–187 give the lie to Richard's previous words and avowed purposes?
7. What is the purpose of 193–207?
8. Is it kindness that dictates the change in the period of banishment, 209–212? How is this effect reinforced by Bolingbroke's answer and by l. 226?
9. How do Gaunt's speeches change after the exit of Richard, and for what reason?
10. With 279–280a compare *Coriolanus*, III, 3, 120–123.
11. Which speaker seems nearer the truth in 258–309? Which speaks the language of youth and which speaks that of age? What memorable passage of two lines do you find here? Memorize it.

I, 4.

1. Compare l. 1a with 23 *ff.* Comment.
2. With 23–36 compare *I Henry IV*, III, 2, 50–54.
3. What two things are accomplished by this scene?

II, 1.

1. With 5–16 compare Matthew Arnold's compressed statement in *Sohrab and Rustum*, "Truth sits upon the lips of dying men." Does Gaunt manage to convey any more meaning in his eleven lines than Sohrab in one? Comment, with this passage as a basis, upon one prime characteristic of Shakespeare's style. Is it simple, compressed, restrained?
*2. Do 21–23 apply primarily to the reign of Richard or to the reigns of Henry VIII and Elizabeth? Do you know of any evidence of Italian influence upon·English literature in the reign of Richard II?
3. What is the dramatic fault in the famous and truly eloquent passage 40–68? For this same dramatic fault, compare *Romeo and Juliet*, I, 4, 53–94, and *As You Like It*, II, 7, 139 *ff.* What would be the effect of the present passage upon an Elizabethan audience? Is this what the poet had in mind, rather than dramatic propriety? Compare I, 3, 159 *ff.*
4. What is the dramatic value and effect of Gaunt's dying prophecy?
5. How does Richard alienate sympathy in this scene?

II, 2.

1. How do the queen's words modify your attitude toward Richard? Do you think 8b–9a is to be interpreted as entirely due to partiality, or does it indicate a phase of Richard's nature that has not yet been shown?
2. How do the queen's words corroborate those of the dying Gaunt, and to what purpose?
3. Comment upon the heavily artificial quality of 1–40.
4. What is the ironic effect of Green's entrance just after l. 40?

5. Does the queen intend a personal reference to those present in 69b–70 ?

6. Source of the pathos in 105 ?

7. From II, 1, 186 *ff.*, and II, 2, 98 *ff.*, estimate the character of York, especially as regards his powers of prompt and efficient action. Is the character vigorously conceived and presented in a convincing and lively fashion, or is it coldly and feebly drawn ?

8. How do the favorites of Richard act in his extremity ? How does this reflect upon the character of the absent king ? By what other means is Richard kept constantly in our minds throughout this scene ?

II, 3.

1. How do 2–18 reflect the character of the speaker ?

2. By what conflicting emotions is York torn in 86 *ff.* ? Compare 158–159a with II, 1, 211, and comment. Explain York's final attitude toward Bolingbroke and his party.

3. Is it possible to respect York after this scene ? What is the exact nature of his sin ? Is it a sin incident chiefly to youth or to age, which makes a merit of seeing two sides of every question ?

II, 4.

1. Purpose of this scene ? Can you remember previous passages having the same purpose ?

2. What passage recalls scenes in *Macbeth* and in *Julius Cæsar* ?

III, 1.

1. Is there an anachronism in l. 24 ?

2. How do 1–30 modify your view of Bolingbroke's character, if at all ?

III, 2.

1. Comment upon 4–26 in any way that seems appropriate. What change in Richard since his last appearance ? What has caused it ?

2. Contrast Richard as shown in 4–26 with Bolingbroke in III, 1, 1–30. Which is the more kingly? Which has the richer mind and the greater personal charm?

3. What great claim of English sovereigns is invoked in 36–62?

4. What irony in 61b–62? Are 83–87a consciously ironical?

5. What growing disease of the mind, illustrated in 93–103, is destroying Richard's powers of action? Compare him, in this respect, with his uncle York. In what very broad and general way is Richard like Hamlet?

6. With 155–156 compare the stage business in *Richard III*, IV, 4, 30 *ff.* What are the approximate dates of the two plays? Do you think these lines a possible reminiscence of the impressive tableau in the earlier play?

7. Compare the spirit and underlying philosophy of 144–177 with those of 36–62. Explain important differences.

8. Would it have mattered to Richard if he had known that he was contradicting himself? What does matter to him and with what is he chiefly concerned in these touching and beautiful lines? His lost kingdom? His dead friends? The vagaries and arabesques of his own fancy?

9. Does Richard here command respect or love? Compare Bolingbroke.

10. Is the character of Aumerle consistently drawn? Compare his speeches in I, 4, with those in this scene.

III, 3.

1. Is there anything surprising in the attitude of York in 7 *ff.*? Explain it.

*2. Is Bolingbroke's duplicity in 31–61 in accord with the facts of history? Is it consistent with the character as drawn?

3. What earlier speech of Richard's is recalled by 72–100? Compare 143–175, as to its psychology and underlying habit of thought, with an earlier speech which it closely resembles. What is the purpose or value of

this parallelism? With 143–175, compare *III Henry
VI*. II, 5, 19 *ff*.

4. What characteristic of Richard's mind causes him to
fall back so suddenly, here and elsewhere, from a
haughty insistence upon the external insignia of power
and royal prerogative to a poetical and sentimental
humility? Why does he seem to know no mean between the two extremes? Has he ever realized the true,
inward essence of real power? Has he a strong sense
of personal worth or of self-respect? What was his
manner of showing power, when he had it, to the world
and to himself?

5. Gather from Richard's speeches in the second half of
the scene evidences of extreme intellectual subtlety and
activity, which increase as his will declines. Note especially 194b–195 and l. 203. Is not the latter line a
complete, exhaustive comment upon York's whole action?

6. What modern philosopher is associated in your mind
with the idea so bitterly and ironically expressed in
200b–201?

III, 4.

1. Do the gardener and his assistants speak in character?
Is the apology in 27–28 adequate?

*2. Compare the poet's treatment of the laboring classes
in somewhat earlier plays: *II Henry VI*, IV, 2;
Love's Labour's Lost, character of Costard; *Two Gentlemen of Verona*, characters of Launce and Speed;
Midsummer Night's Dream, the Bottom group; *Merchant of Venice*, character of Launcelot; *Taming of
the Shrew*, character of Sly.

3. Note that the laborers are not introduced for comic
effect (this may be partially due to the influence of
Marlowe) and that they are attached to one of the noblest families in England. Would a treatment of them
more in accord with the poet's general practice have
harmonized well with the tragic and pathetic treatment
of the queen?

4. Basing your judgment upon the above citations and upon the present passage, should you say that Shakespeare's frequently contemptuous treatment of the lower classes was due to personal convictions or to the exigencies of his dramatic purpose?

5. What is the purpose of this discussion of great public affairs by the common people? Compare *Richard III*, II, 3, *Julius Cæsar*, III, 3, and *Macbeth*, II, 4.

IV, 1.

1. As a matter of history, Bolingbroke actually assisted Richard in his aggressions against the Duke of Gloucester. Does Act I of this play give the impression that Gloucester's assassination and Bolingbroke's banishment occurred at nearly the same time, as 10–19 seem to indicate?

2. With 14–19 compare I, 4, 1–19.

3. In order to realize the poet's care with subordinate characters, recall the impression made by Aumerle in previous scenes.

4. Comment upon the stage effect of 19–85. Since this action is not completed, why does it find place here? Since the Bishop of Carlisle's prophecy is not fulfilled in this play, for what purposes was it written? Compare *II Henry IV*, IV, 5, 184 *ff*.

5. Comment upon the truth of York's striking expression, "tired majesty," l. 178. How far does this go toward explaining Richard's manner?

6. What seems to be the attitude of York in this scene?

7. Comment upon the historical accuracy of l. 263.

8. By what means does Richard win our love and, perhaps, even some measure of respect in this very powerful scene?

9. In what ways does this scene seem to be fitted for strong stage effect?

V, 1.

1. Explain the apparent coldness of "fair woman" and "good soul," 16 and 17. Does Richard express here

an overwhelming sorrow? Does this add to the pathos
of the scene?

V, 2.

1. Why is Shakespeare content merely to indicate the
   queen's future life? Should attention be centered here
   upon Richard or upon his queen? Why?
2. Comment upon 23–26.
3. What preparation has there been for the revelation of
   the conspiracy against the king?
4. Point out contrasts between father, mother, and son.
   Can you trace the son's characteristics in his parents?
5. What elements make for a peculiar liveliness in this
   scene?
*6. Do the Duke and Duchess show the typical and normal
   attitudes of father and mother respectively toward an
   erring son who is in danger of his life? Compare
   Mother Asa's attitude, under similar circumstances, in
   Ibsen's *Peer Gynt.*

V, 3.

1. How do 1–12a link this play with the principal interest of the Henry IV plays?
2. Are there evidences that the poet found it hard to reconcile the pardoning of Aumerle with Bolingbroke's
   character as he had conceived it and with the disclo-
   sures of IV, 1? Is this one of the few places in which
   his stubborn historical material, very closely followed
   in this play, is not bent entirely to his purpose?
3. Why is this scene so much less interesting and convincing than the preceding? Comment especially upon the
   slow movement and the anti-climax of 87–146.

V, 5.

1. What two passages of Scripture are vaguely recalled
   in 15–17? Is there a real contradiction between them?
   Do 11–17 mean that one must not think deeply upon
   " things divine " if he is to avoid the discovery of fatal
   contradictions even in Holy Writ itself? Does Richard

seem the sort of man to whom a simple faith is easy and natural?

2. What evidence, in 1–66, of an increase in Richard's intellectual disease?

3. By what means does the poet lessen the shock (and the danger to the success of his play) in this representation of the assassination of an English king?

V, 6.

1. Does the drama end "upon a note of rest"? What prophecies, actions, forebodings, are left incomplete? Is this a fault, or is it due to the very nature of the chronicle play, as such? What does it indicate regarding the poet's plans for future work?

2. What is done in this scene to round out the action as far as possible?

HENRY IV, PART I

GENERAL QUESTIONS

1. Enumerate the actions and the groups of characters. Divide these actions and groups into two broad and general classes. By what character are the two divisions connected?

2. What is the main action and what the main group of characters? Why do you say so? What action and what group constantly threatens the predominance of the main action and the main group? Is this a fault? Can you explain it? State and defend your choice as to the hero of the play.

3. Does this play make an effect of unity? Is such unity as it has achieved by mechanical means, as in *The Winter's Tale*, or is it pervading and intrinsic, as in *Othello*? In what ways is it evident that the poet's shaping power is embarrassed by the stubborn facts of history?

4. Is the effect of this play primarily that of a chronicle play, a tragedy, or a comedy? What elements of each of these does it possess? To which form did the poet intend to shape it? How was he led astray?

5. Cite several examples of character contrast. Show that this device makes for economy in characterization.

6. Do you think Hal or Hotspur the larger and better man? Give definite reasons. What did the poet think? Do you find his method of showing his preference adequate, artistic, convincing? How much weight did he put upon Hal's victory over Hotspur on the battlefield?

7. Did Shakespeare's audience feel regarding the members of the Falstaff group that they were men of the early fifteenth century or that they were men of contemporary, late-sixteenth-century London? How would

this affect the feeling of the audience toward the purely historical matter ?

8. Write a study of Falstaff in not less than five hundred words, discussing the following points: Is Falstaff a coward ? Why does he cultivate Hal and why does Hal permit him to do so ? Was he wholly studied from life, wholly imagined, or "compounded of many simples"? What is meant in calling him one of the three or four greatest creations among the characters of Shakespeare's plays?

9. How is this play connected with *Richard II*? What would you think of an attempt to use the play as an historical document? How much effort does the poet make to depict the life and customs of the opening fifteenth century rather than those of his own day ?

10. What gave the play its extraordinary popularity in Shakespeare's time ? Why is it so much less popular on the stage to-day ? It is almost impossible to render faithfully a play of the chronicle type on the modern stage. The jaded audiences of to-day lag pitifully behind Falstaff's galloping wit. Moreover, the modern audience, which Puritanism has "blown gray with its breath," is bewildered by this Gargantuan figure of a gross fat man who lives by thievery and sack, but who must, nevertheless, be admired.

DETAILED QUESTIONS

I, 1.

1. The battle of Holmedon occurred in September of 1402. Richard II died in January of 1400. With line 28 compare *Richard II*, V, 6, 49–50. What advantage is gained by this slight modification of history ?

2. What were Henry's reasons for wishing to undertake a Crusade ? See the closing lines of *Richard II*. Are 1–33 spoken in perfect sincerity ? Does it seem likely that the king does not already know the substance of what Westmoreland reports in 34–46 and 49–61 ? How

does his show of ignorance serve the poet's purpose in this scene?

3. In the light of later developments in the scene, what dramatic irony do you find in 5–18a?

4. With 18b–33 compare *II Henry IV*, IV, 5, 232–241.

5. Note that the first speech of the play is given to the king and compare the first speeches of *King John*, *Richard III*, *Richard II*, and *Henry V*. Comment.

6. Characterize the diction of 1–33.

7. Note throughout the remainder of the scene the introduction of the names of persons absent and the characterization of each. Why is this done? What two persons are most carefully characterized and by what means?

8. What exposition is given in this later portion of the scene over and above mere characterization?

*9. What were the actual ages of Hotspur and Prince Hal in 1402? What was the age of the king? How does the poet represent their ages? Compare V, 1, 13. Why does he do this?

10. With 77 *ff.* compare *Richard II*, V, 3, 1–12a.

11. What feature of the political and social conditions of the early fifteenth century made Hotspur's withholding of the prisoners a more venial offense than it would have been in the time of Elizabeth?

I, 2.

1. Explain the change to prose. What is the effect of this change?

2. After reading a few lines of this scene, try to give a reason for the style of the speeches in scene 1, especially that of the king's first speech. Or is this latter only the conventional style of Shakespeare's kings? Compare the first speech of *Richard III*.

3. What is the point of 2–9? Note the repetition of the word "day" and Falstaff's rejoinder.

4. Paraphrase 26–33.

5. How do 47–48a recall a phase of the early history of this play?

6. Read aloud many times 89–98 and 101–109. Be prepared to render them so as to show the peculiar rhythm
of Falstaff's speech as well as the kaleidoscopic shifts
and doublings of his thought. What single sentence in
these two speeches seems to you the most delightfully
characteristic of the speaker?

7. Would it have been well to have used another name
for the character Gadshill, since the place Gadshill is
to be so prominently mentioned? But how did the
character probably come by the name? The error, if it
is one, goes back to the *Famous Victories of Henry V*,
which Shakespeare used to some extent as a source.

8. How do the epithets in 177–178 apply to Falstaff?

9. Is the character of the prince effectively shielded by
making him join the robbers not for the sake of the
theft but for the sake of the jest? Has not the prince
been guilty of robbery in that he has been associating
with thieves? Is it morally or dramatically a different
thing to show him on the stage as actually participat-
ing in a robbery? Which is more important here, the
moral or the dramatic aspect of the matter? Why?

10. Discuss the dramatic value of 218–240. How does it
prepare for *II Henry IV*, V, 5? Granting the necessity of this material, can you suggest a more artistic
way of presenting it?

11. Is this soliloquy convincing and has it the effect of sincerity? Does Hal give satisfying reasons for his mode
of life or is he merely devising an argument to quiet
his conscience? Consider, in this connection, the immediate context. Do you like to feel that Hal is giving
himself only half-heartedly and out of policy to the wild
life in which we see him? What effect would such a
feeling have upon your pleasure in the comic portions
of the play?

12. Prince Hal was to become Shakespeare's ideal man of
action. The chronicles base upon feebly founded tradition a report that Hal was wild and dissolute in his
youth. Do you think this much-vexed soliloquy may
be explained as the poet's not entirely successful at-

tempt to reconcile the contradiction and to present Hal's life as an unbroken and harmonious whole? Or may there be an autobiographical tinge in these lines — some vague recollection of the poet's own youth at Stratford and the vows there made? Note that one chief reason, not expressed in the present passage, for Hal's pleasure in low life is his desire to know all sorts and conditions of men. It is certain that the same desire must have taken the poet many times into even stranger company.

13. What family likeness is discernible between Hal as shown in these lines and his father as revealed in III, 2, 29 *ff.*?

I, 3.

1. How does Worcester's outbreak and dismissal prepare for his action later in the scene? Does he deliberately attempt to anger the king? Compare 272–276.

2. What is the effect of the alliteration in 50–55?

3. Point out in 30–64 several instances of " convincing detail " — minor details which could not be readily imagined and would be observed only by an alert witness, and which give, therefore, an air of realistic fidelity to the whole report.

4. By what indirect and highly successful method is Hotspur's character developed in these lines? Briefly outline his character as delineated in 29–69. Do you know more or less about him after this speech than you do about Hal after I, 2? Why is this?

5. Is there any evidence in this scene that the king is trying to fabricate a case against Mortimer? Compare 81–82 with 114. Why should he do so? Compare 145–150. What actions of Mortimer's lend color to the king's charge?

6. With l. 83 compare 116–117. Why does the king fear Glendower? Contrast III, 1, 13–62, and 148–164.

7. What is the part played by Worcester in 139 *ff.*? What is he trying to do?

8. Contrast Hotspur, Worcester, and Northumberland in

the rest of this scene, as to subtlety, impetuosity, nobility of character. By what means is the superior moral and personal power of Hotspur made evident? What motives actuate Hotspur in joining the rebellion?

9. With 242–248 compare II, 4, 373, III, 1, 5–6, and *Coriolanus*, I. 9, 82–92. Compare also *Julius Cæsar*, IV, 3, 252–253. What is the effect of these passages?

10. Point out the passages of vivid lyrical poetry in Hotspur's speeches in this scene. Comment upon character portrayal in the beautiful rant of 201–205. In what moods and upon what subjects is Hotspur a poet? Is this consistent with III, 1, 127–135?

II, 1.

1. To what elements does the scene between the carriers owe its charm? Would it seem to Shakespeare's audience to have taken place in 1402 or to be contemporary? What effect would this have upon their feeling regarding the historical characters and incidents of the play?

*2. Are there scenes in other Shakespearean plays that deal in this intensely realistic manner with the low life of London? Present evidence that Shakespeare was more or was less interested in such material than his fellow dramatists, Jonson, Dekker, Chapman, Heywood.

3. Why are the companions of Falstaff and Hal not made illiterate?

4. Purpose of this scene? What scenes does it link? How does it bridge the gap in tone and feeling between I, 3, and II, 2?

II, 2.

1. How is Falstaff held in the center of interest even when not present on the stage?

2. Does Falstaff play the coward in this scene? Compare him in this respect with Gadshill, Bardolph, and Peto.

3. Out of what material does Falstaff make humor? Note especially 10–29, 36–40, and 80–90. Does he laugh more at others than at himself? Is this humility or supreme egoism?

II, 3.

1. What characteristics of Hotspur, shown in 1–38, are similar to those revealed in I, 3, 125–302 ?

2. What purposes, apart from characterization, are served by the reading of the letter ?

3. Does Lady Percy's description of Hotspur's overwrought condition indicate fear, on his part, of the outcome, or what ? A professional soldier whose whole life has been lived under arms, why should he be so excited now ? Is there anything exceptional in his present situation ?

4. With this scene compare *Julius Cæsar*, II, 1, 233–309. What is the difference in tone and to what is the difference due ? What is the difference in outcome ? If possible, show that in either case the wife's character is a reflection of the husband's.

5. What grave defects of Hotspur's character are shown here ? Are they consistent with what we already know of him ?

6. What premonition and vague preparation is suggested here of the outcome of the rebellion ? •

II, 4.

1. Can you think of any justification for Hal's association with tapsters in order to learn their language and their outlook on life ? Contrast him with his father as shown in III, 2, 29 *ff*. Does your explanation account for his association with Falstaff and his fellows ? Are these latter on the same level with the tapsters ?

2. What is the "issue" of the jest upon Francis ? Are 104–107 an answer ? Is it a good jest ? Would it be bettered in acting ? Can you see any reason for making the scene up to the entrance of Falstaff a little dull ?

*3. Study, if possible in Schmidt's *Shakespeare Lexicon*, the poet's use of the word "humor," l. 104, before and after 1598, the date of Ben Jonson's *Every Man in His Humour*.

*4. Compare the style of 110–121 with that of the "character-writing" that came into vogue a decade after this play was published and which was, to some extent, an outgrowth of the interest in "humors." Compare *Twelfth Night*, I, 5, 165–171, and *Troilus and Cressida*, I, 2, 20–31. Note that the latter passage is perhaps a covert satire upon the father of the "humors," Ben Jonson.

5. What association of ideas leads Hal on in the same breath from Francis to Hotspur? Is it that in considering his mastery of all humors he suddenly thinks of Hotspur as one of the most notable in his whole range of experience? Or is he contrasting his own pleasure in humorous observation of life and slow storing of experience with Hotspur's precocious quest of violent action?

6. Compare, for justice, knowledge, and good humor, Hal's treatment of Hotspur in 115–121 with Hotspur's attitude toward Hal as shown in I, 3, 230–233, IV, 1, 94b–97a, and IV, 1, 111–112a. Compare also V, 1, 85b–100, and V, 2, 46 *ff*.

7. What preparation in 121b–123a?

8. What has been the purpose of Poins and Hal in tricking Falstaff? Compare I, 2, 207–213. Do they take pleasure, in 126–312, in proving Falstaff a liar or in the ingenuity of his lies? Does Falstaff know this? Give evidence that he does or that he does not expect to be believed in the story he tells.

9. Where, in this passage, is Falstaff at the height of his enjoyment and of his wit? Is it in those places where he is most clearly detected in his lies and where the demand is greatest upon his ingenuity? Select passages of special brilliancy in which the wit does not play upon the immediate situation.

10. With 143–145a compare 364–365 and I, 2, 101–106. What similarity in these passages?

11. In 321–322 we have the only reference to Queen Joan, Hal's stepmother. In *Richard II* Shakespeare falsified history in order to bring Richard's queen, in reality a child of nine, into the play. Why does he refrain from presenting the wife of Henry?

12. What is the source of humor in 325–328? Compare II, 2, 89.

13. Considering that this scene is very long, what is the value of the interpolation of matter from the serious plot in 362–412? How is this material made to harmonize with the tone of the scene? Is some violence done to the character of Hal in this necessary harmonization? What advance has been made in the rebellion since we last heard of it?

14. Note the natural and easy leading-up to the "play-extempore" in 410–412 and the preparation for it in 308–309 and 121–122.

15. Why do we not blame the prince, whose "father's beard is turned white" with anxiety and whose succession to the throne is endangered, for the unfilial frivolity of this scene? Is it because we are dominated, as Hal is also for the nonce, by the spirit of comedy, or rather the spirit of Falstaff, before which nothing is sacred?

16. Find other instances in the remainder of the scene of this subjection of all dissonances to the one compelling comic theme. How far does this go toward condoning l. 561?

17. Point out, in 438 ff., several parodies of the style of John Lyly's *Euphues*. Setting aside the obvious anachronism, discuss the propriety of making such a man as Falstaff burlesque a style of speech affected only at the court and in fashionable society. Is he a man of wide reading and intellectual culture? Are we to judge him, any more conclusively than we do the prince, by the low society in which we find him?

18. Do you think Falstaff is somewhat more serious in his *apologia pro vita sua* in 512–527 than in 463–475? Compare 531–533 and 539–541.

19. With 599–600 compare III, 3, 199–200.

III, 1.

1. Enumerate the contrasts presented in this scene between the Anglo-Saxon and the Celtic temperament. What characteristics of the Welsh are represented by Glendower?

2. Point out several passages dealing with the difficulty of the Welsh language.

3. Are the contrasts between Hotspur and Glendower all deeply rooted in character and racial differences or are some of them due to differences in their respective ways of expressing themselves? Is Hotspur less self-assertive than Glendower or only less outspoken in his self-esteem? See 13–69. Does Hotspur feel less intensely than Glendower or has he the Anglo-Saxon's sentimental fear of emotional display? See 192–271.

4. Which of the two seems to you on the whole the more admirable — Glendower, with his expansive and ingenuous egotism, his universal curiosity, his wide experience in action, art, and learning, and most of all his patience and forbearance, or Hotspur, with his intolerant, carefully hidden egotism, his hatred of the arts and of all illusion — when seen in others? Can Hotspur deal in sentimental illusion also when on one of the few subjects in which he is interested? Compare the famous lines, I, 3, 201–205.

5. Supposing that Shakespeare judged the two at all, which do you think he found the more to his mind? See 127–135. Compare *A Midsummer Night's Dream*, V, 1, 2–22. Is Hotspur condemning poetry or versification in this passage? Do you recall passages in which he is himself a poet? Comment, in this connection, upon the powerful phrasing of 96–105.

6. What part is played by Mortimer and Worcester in this scene? Upon what ground does Worcester base his reproof of Hotspur in 177 *ff.*? How is this characteristic?

7. What would be the effect upon the sympathies of an English audience of the scene dealing with the partition of the kingdom?

8. What feeling is left by this scene regarding the probable success of the Percy rebellion? What preparation is made for Glendower's later action? Compare IV, 4, 18.

III, 2.

1. Contrast the characters of father and son in this scene. Why does not the father understand his son? Does the lack of understanding seem due to the father's fault or to the son's?

2. What new elements in the character of each are developed? By what means is this made possible?

3. Does the king anywhere complain of Hal's conduct as immoral, or on any other than grounds of policy? Comment. Does the scene in any way resemble that rehearsed the night before in the tavern? In what manner does Hal meet his father's charges?

4. Is Hal's vow to kill Hotspur any extenuation, at least according to modern standards, of what has been morally wrong in his own past action? Does he intend it as such? Why, then, does the king accept it with such apparent satisfaction? Is there a suggestion here of the old idea of trial by battle?

5. What advantage is derived here from the well-established idea of rivalry between Hal and Hotspur? To what character in the play is this idea most frequently present?

III, 3.

1. Show that the humor of this scene is derived from sources and materials similar to those employed in II, 4.

2. Is Falstaff at all serious in his accusations of the hostess? Does he expect to extract money from her on such a pretext? With l. 69 and 133–134 compare Dr. Johnson's retort upon the railing fish-wife in calling her a "parallelopiped." What character is given its first careful treatment in this scene?

3. What, if anything, is implied as to Hal's sincerity in III, 2, by his presence among his old companions immediately after that scene? Comment especially upon 203–204.

4. Into what parts is the scene divided? How do the first

parts prepare for the last? Why does not Hal appear in the first parts?

5. Explain the change to verse in l. 225.

IV, 1.

1. Explain 10–12, and especially the exact connotation of " so potent."

2. Is there any slight evidence that Worcester understands the nature of Northumberland's sickness better than Hotspur? How is this characteristic? Compare *II Henry IV*, Induction, 36–37a.

3. Compare Hotspur's reception of the letter with that given to the letter from the unnamed correspondent in II, 3, 1–38. Note a similar trick of manner in l. 31 of this scene.

4. Do 44–52 seem the sort of argument you would expect from Hotspur? Explain it.

5. Paraphrase 61–62a. Comment upon 62b–65. Why does Worcester see this so clearly?

6. Does Vernon speak, in 97b–103, of the comrades of the prince with whom we are acquainted?

7. For what purpose is this glowing praise of Hal given, at just this point, from the mouth of an enemy? Compare V, 2, 52–69. Note the contrast of Hotspur's attitude in both passages. Is there any person besides Vernon in the play who sees Hal in this light? What is the value of Vernon's testimony as a transition from the Prince Hal of the Boar's Head Tavern to the Prince Henry of Wales on the field of Shrewsbury?

8. Is there anything in 111–124a that still further alienates sympathy from Hotspur? Does he hope for victory after 124b–126?

9. Enumerate the ways in which the defeat of the Percy rebellion has been prepared for in this and earlier scenes.

10. What part is played by Worcester and Douglas in this scene? What is the range of Douglas's intellectual horizon? Compare him, in this respect, with Hotspur. What is the effect of his presence in the play upon your

feeling toward Hotspur? Compare the dramatic function of Tybalt in *Romeo and Juliet*.

IV, 2.

1. Why does Falstaff appear in a less favorable light in this than in any previous scene? Does the Prince see this? What effect does it have upon him?
2. What principles of the Falstaffian philosophy — principles expounded in V, 1, 127 *ff.*, and V, 4, 111 *ff.* — partially explain his action?
3. Do you recall, in the world's literature, another such complete, compact, and final exposure of the folly of war as is found in 71–74? Falstaff probably intends no more here than one of his humorous evasions of a moral issue, but, in making this, he punctures the most monstrous fallacy of the ages.

IV, 3.

1. Comment upon the speeches of Douglas in the first fourteen lines.
2. Characterize Hotspur's rehearsal of his grievances in 52–105. What is the value of this recapitulation of historic facts so late in the play?
3. What is the character and attitude of Blunt? Compare I, 1, 62–63. Does he pay allegiance to the person or to the office of the king?

IV, 4.

1. What would be lost to the play in the elimination of this scene? Note that the Archbishop of York is a leader in the second rebellion, which is a main theme of *II Henry IV*.
2. The three preceding scenes and all the scenes of Act V are laid out of doors and were set on the fore-stage. Comment.

V, 1.

1. With 1–8 compare *Richard III*, V, 4, 282–287.
2. Is Worcester telling the truth in 25b–26?
3. Comment upon 28–29.

4. Does the presence of Falstaff in this group of the highest men in the realm seem natural? Compare IV, 2, 54 *ff.*, and *II Henry IV*, III, 2, 27–29.

5. What does Hal gain by respecting and praising his rival? Compare V, 4, 72–73.

6. Does the king gain or lose in royal dignity by his offer of pardon at the last moment? Here, as in the preceding question and everywhere, an answer of vague and vapid moralizing is of no value. Both questions are dramatic and not ethical in bearing.

7. The charges made in IV, 3, and in this scene against Henry IV are historically valid. Many persons in Shakespeare's audience would have known this. What considerations are set against these charges so as to retain sympathy for the royal party?

8. Are there slight indications of a change in Hal's attitude toward Falstaff? Or do you think he does no more than express here thoughts which he has had from the beginning? Why should he express them under the present circumstances? Does Falstaff seem in his element in this scene?

9. Is it cowardice or a sort of ignoble common sense that inspires Falstaff's famous catechism, 127–144? How much of his reasoning is sound and convincing?

10. A great deal is said in this play about honor and reputation, which may be likened, in its relation to the drama, to a musical theme sounded in several different keys. In this soliloquy we have the humorous inversion of that theme. It is said that we know nothing fully and truly, not even the most sacred thing, until we can laugh at it. State the varying relations toward this central theme of the king, the prince, Hotspur, Glendower, Falstaff, and Douglas.

V, 2.

1. Why does Worcester falsify the king's message? How is this action in character?

2. Is Hotspur sincere in saying that he "has not well the gift of tongue," or does he say this with the same in-

tent that actuates Antony in *Julius Cæsar*, III, 2,
221 ? Does his speech to the soldiers prove the statement true? Why is it that Shakespeare, with all the
immense range of his characters, has nowhere presented
a character of any importance that is deficient in the
power of speech? Even Caliban has a command of
language which might be envied by an orator. Is
Silence an exception ?

3. Are your sympathies with the rebels or with the king's
party at the close of this scene ? With Hal or with
Hotspur? Why?

V, 3.

1. Does the poet mean to imply that Douglas is a better
man than Blunt — except perhaps in strength of wrist
and biceps — because he kills him? How does this
bear upon the rivalry between Hotspur and Hal and
its outcome?

2. How and why is Falstaff made to suffer by being presented in the midst of action and by not having the
center of the stage to himself as in previous scenes?
What effect does his presence here have upon your
feeling toward these battle scenes?

3. How does Hal's manner toward Falstaff, in 41–58,
differ from that to which we have become accustomed?
How is it that Hal can change so radically in this regard while Falstaff cannot, or at least does not?

V, 4.

1. What is the poet's purpose in introducing the theme of
the valor of Prince John?

2. Since this is a play of Henry IV, the king should be
the hero of Shrewsbury. Holinshed makes him so.
Does Shakespeare? Why ?

3. What is the artistic purpose in presenting, side by
side with the death-grapple between the two rivals
towards which the action of the entire play has been
directed, a farcical conflict between the butcher Douglas and the philosophic Falstaff, whose opinions upon
the subject of " honor " have been recently expressed?

4. Napoleon Bonaparte, with this play in mind, is reported as saying that Shakespeare seemed to have the childish idea that the relative worth of two men could be accurately determined by the cut and thrust of sword-play. Discuss this point fully. By what means has Hal been shown to be the better man, aside from this present conflict? Was physical strength an insignificant thing in 1402? Is it even now, when the puniest man can at least pull a trigger? Is it sufficient to say that Hal, having shown himself the better man in all other respects, here meets and defeats his rival on his own ground?

*5. Discuss the mediæval theory of "trial by battle" in its relations to the fight between Hal and Hotspur. Compare *Richard II*, I, 1, *passim*.

6. What is the exact nature of Hal's feeling for Falstaff as presented in 102–110? Is there anything in this speech to reinforce the soliloquy in I, 2, 218 *ff.*?

7. Falstaff has enjoyed a privilege accorded to but few — he has overheard a friend mourning his death. He should know, now, precisely what Hal thinks of him. What is the nature of his reaction?

8. Is there any possibility that Falstaff expects his lie about the killing of Hotspur to be believed? What bearing has this upon the motive of his other lies, in II, 4?

9. What is gained by Hal's agreeing to lie for Falstaff?

V, 5.

1. Is the play rounded off and all the actions completed with this scene? Why?

HENRY IV, PART II

GENERAL QUESTIONS

1. Answer for this play questions 1–4 on *Henry IV, Part I*.
2. How is this play connected with *Part I*? Do you think the two parts were planned together, or was the second part an afterthought? How does the second part compare, in interest, with the first? Give reasons for this. What new material is added to enhance interest?
3. Collect all passages in this and the preceding play that serve as preparation for the change in Hal's manner of life and in his attitude toward his former associates. Has the poet succeeded in rationalizing this change?
4. Discuss the reasons for Hal's rejection of Falstaff. How has this rejection been prepared for? Is the poet fair to Falstaff? Does Falstaff get "poetic justice"? Is Falstaff treated with perfect consistency throughout the two plays? Are the Falstaff scenes as good in this part as in the first?
5. If you were preparing an acting version of *Henry IV* for the modern stage and were confined to five acts, would you select the entire first part, the entire second part, or separate acts and scenes from each? Give reasons.
6. Make a selection and arrangement of acts and scenes from the two plays that will form a distinct play, as unified and coherent as possible and covering the essential historical matter of the two plays while preserving the most interesting Falstaff scenes.

DETAILED QUESTIONS

INDUCTION

1. Argue from the style and thought of Rumour's speech that this passage was or was not written by Shakespeare.

2. What is the dramatic purpose of the speech? Might this purpose have been served more artistically in some other way?

3. Explain Shakespeare's gradual abandonment of prologues and introductory soliloquies, commonly employed by his predecessors and contemporaries.

I, 1.

1. Character of Northumberland in this scene? Comment upon his speeches, especially 67–81.

2. Value of Lord Bardolph's false report from Shrewsbury?

3. What exposition in this scene? How does it link the second to the first part?

I, 2.

1. What should be said of the self-respect shown in 7–11a? Illustrate, by reference to events in *Part I*, the truth of 11b–13a.

2. How does the poet betray the workings of his own art in 13b–16a?

3. Is Falstaff talking to the Page in 7–34, or does this speech amount to a soliloquy?

4. In what several ways does 61–254 connect the present with the preceding play? What exposition in this passage? How does it forward the action?

5. Cite several passages of especial brilliance in Falstaff's encounter with the Chief Justice. Characterize his attitude toward the Chief Justice in one word.

6. Comment closely upon the last sentence of the scene as highly characteristic of the speaker.

I, 3.

1. What premonition as to the outcome of the second rebellion is given by this scene: (*a*) by what is said and what is already known, from *Part I*, about the character of Northumberland; (*b*) by the character and words of Lord Bardolph?

2. What is the effect upon your sympathies of 85–108?

Cite similar pronouncements upon a similar theme from other Shakespearean plays. What, exactly, are the charges Northumberland makes against the "fond many"?

II, 1.

1. What two conflicting emotions are manifested in the Hostess's speeches, 1–45?
2. With the subtlety and cutting edge of the Hostess's repartee in 53–55, compare II, 4, 79–114, and *Part I*, III, 3, 74–75, 135–136a, 146–148.
3. Where has the Hostess acquired her vocabulary of abuse? Does she address Falstaff or the Page as "Hemp-seed"? Which would give the better comic effect?
4. Does Falstaff show any sign of being daunted by the entrance of the Chief Justice and his men, which creates perhaps the most trying situation in which we have seen the fat knight? Just how does he extricate himself?
5. Comment closely upon the association of ideas exhibited in 91–112. What important element is lacking in the Hostess's process of thought? Does the great mass of "convincing detail" which she piles up really carry conviction that Falstaff had promised to marry her? What words toward the close of the speech come near to clinching the truth of the whole?
6. Compare this speech closely with *Romeo and Juliet*, I, 3, 16–48. With Mistress Quickly's style of invective, compare II, 4, 158–181, of the same play.
7. Compare this quarrel, as to its cause, Falstaff's conduct in it and its outcome, with that in *Part I*, III, 3, 60 *ff*.

II, 2.

1. Under what circumstances and in what mood was Hal last seen? How do 1–74 serve to bridge the gap? Comment upon the underlying significance of line 1. Does Poins show the discernment of real friendship in 31–32?
2. What passages do you find in Hal's speeches, 1–74,

serving the same purpose as *Part I*, I, 2, 218–240, to those in Shakespeare's audience who might be unfamiliar with the earlier play?

3. How much does the poet depend in this scene upon a knowledge of *Part I*? What does this indicate regarding his audiences?

4. How much truth do you find in Hal's half-ironical words: "Thou art a blessed fellow to think as every man thinks"? Do they apply in any way to the speaker's life and character?

*5. Comment upon the speeches of the Page. Compare them with those of Mamillius in *The Winter's Tale* or of Arthur in *King John* or of the two children of Clarence in *Richard III*.

6. What evidence that Hal and Falstaff are less intimate than formerly? Does Falstaff's letter show that he realizes this?

7. What exposition having to do with the serious plot in this scene?

II, 3.

1. With 18–32a compare *Hamlet*, III, 1, 158–162, and *Antony and Cleopatra*, V, 2, 76–92. What is the common element in the loves of these three women?

2. What is Lady Percy's real reason for wishing to keep Northumberland from the war? Is her argument a good one?

3. Compare this scene, as to its outcome, with *Part I*, II, 3. Contrast the attitudes of father and son towards women. Why, probably, did Northumberland fail to appear at Shrewsbury?

4. What scenes are linked by this scene? What augury for the rebellion is indicated?

II, 4.

1. With 1–10 compare *Part I*, III, 3, 1–5.

2. Arrange 70b–73a in rhyme and rhythm.

3. Compare 77b–78a with 137–143 and 150–163. Does there seem to be a slight suspicion of "swaggering"

in Doll's mode of speech? Does she really hate Pistol
as she says? If so, should she not be able to produce
a less fantastic reason than that he is a "swaggering
rascal" and is "foul-mouthed"? Compare V, 4, 17–19.
What reasons for dissimulation might she have here?

4. What psychological peculiarity of the Hostess is shown
   in 79–118? Is there anything in common between her
   mental processes here and those presented in II, 1,
   92–112?

5. What is the "humor" of Pistol? From what source
   has he gathered his vocabulary? What is characteristic
   in his paraphrase of the famous rant from *Tamburlaine*?
   Do you think this echo of stilted, artificial Marlovian
   tragedy was introduced with any special purpose into
   this broadest Rabelaisian scene of English low comedy?

6. What is the evidence in this scene as to Falstaff's al-
   leged cowardice?

7. How does Falstaff's evasion in 345 *ff.* compare in brilliancy with those of *Part I*? What is the chief pleasure of Poins and Hal in these attempts to corner the
   knight? With 305–306 compare *Part I*, II, 4, 1–97.

8. Give two reasons why the Hostess does not complete
   her sentence in 412–415.

9. Note the intrusion of the outer world at the end of the
   scene. Compare *Part I*, II, 4, and III, 3. What is the
   artistic, or, perhaps, moral effect of thi ?

10. This is one of the most riotously comic scenes in Eng-
    lish literature and it justifies George Meredith's words
    about Shakespeare: "He had a laugh . . . broad as ten
    thousand beeves at pasture." Try to enumerate the ele-
    ments that contribute to the marvelous richness and va-
    riety of the scene. How much is due to broad character
    contrast? How much to the mere rough-and-tumble of
    high animal spirits? How much to obvious or subtle
    gradations and contrasts of peculiarities in diction and
    in use of the English language? How much to setting?

11. Does it seem to you possible that the man who con-
    ceived this scene and lived with delight into every line
    of it was a wizened, ascetic person, an æsthete, or a

pedant? Is it not clear that he must have been a man
with a large margin of physical vitality and a goodly
capacity for sherris-sack?

III, 1.

1. Can you account for the great poetic beauty of 4–31?
Do you think it lies chiefly in the sensuous beauty of
the versification, in the succession of images, in the situation, or in all three perfectly harmonized? Note the
low, murmuring monotony of 7–8 and 10–14. Study
carefully the alliteration upon sibilants in 8–14, upon
u in 10–15 and upon *l* in 14–17. Explain, as far as
possible, the effect secured in each case. Do not suppose, however, that these niceties are the result of conscious effort on the poet's part. Do not suppose that
this "murdering to dissect" will bring you even a little
nearer to the mysterious, hidden soul of poetry.

*2. What is there in 18–25 to justify Matthew Arnold's
choice of the passage as one of his "touchstones" of
high poetic excellence? (See the essay *On the Study
of Poetry*, General Introduction to Ward's *English
Poets*, and reprinted in *Mixed Essays*.) Do you think
it is true of this, as of Arnold's other selections, that
the effect of the passage is largely dependent upon
the context and that therefore it fails as a "touchstone"?

    Collect from Elizabethan sonnets as many treatments
of the theme of Sleep as possible. See list given in
F. E. Schelling's *The Elizabethan Lyric*. Compare
Macbeth, II, 2, 35 *ff.*

3. Read 4–31 aloud many times, committing it to memory
meanwhile if possible, until you are able not only to
understand and to feel but also to interpret all its poetic
values. This may not be the only way, but it is certainly
one of the surest ways of growing to understand the
inner meaning of great poetry. It furnishes the supreme
test of achievement in literary study and is by very
much more difficult than it seems. To this assignment
you should give not less than half an hour.

4. What evidence that King Henry is not meeting this rebellion as he did that of the Percies? Why?

5. With 45–51a compare sonnet 64.

6. With 70–77 compare *Richard II*, V, 1, 55–65. This is perhaps the only place in which the poet quotes *verbatim* from another play written by himself. But note that it is carelessly done, since Bolingbroke was already king when Richard pronounced these words, and neither Bolingbroke nor Warwick was present at the scene in the tower.

7. Under what circumstances and in what moods does Henry remember his vow to go on a crusade, as here, in 107–108? Is he prompted by religious impulse or is his promise a sort of bribe or promise-to-pay, driving a bargain with the Deity? See also IV, 5, 210–213.

III, 2.

1. Enumerate the character contrasts in this scene. How are the mannerisms and characteristics of Shallow designed to set off the figure of Falstaff? What contrasts in peculiarities of speech are presented?

2. What is the relation between this scene and *Part I*, IV, 2?

3. Falstaff soliloquizes more than any other character in Shakespeare's plays, with the exception of Hamlet. What sort of pleasure does he take in it? What does he talk about? Can you reconcile his enjoyment of soliloquy with his character as a lover of good company and of word-fence with a worthy antagonist? To whom are his witticisms addressed in 89–320?

4. Falstaff, like Shallow, has fondly preserved the memories of his youth. The contrast between his juvenile tastes and his gray hairs is a source of constant glee to his companions, who call him " latter-spring " and " All-Hallown Summer." Why, then, does he make cruel sport of Shallow for this same trait? What, if any, is the difference between the two young old men in this respect?

IV, 1.

1. What is the chief oratorical merit of 30–52?
2. Do you think the Archbishop's noble speech a sufficient apology for the appearance of a churchman in arms? Why was such an apology more necessary in Shakespeare's time than in the actual days of Henry IV?
3. The Archbishop's manner being so assured and his speech so sound in thought and phrase, do you not feel that he must have much right on his side? History shows that he had. Why has not the poet allowed us to see more of the king's injustice and more of the rebels' real grievances?
4. With 141–146 compare *Part I*, V, 1, 106–108.
5. Comment upon the power of expression shown in 197–214. Paraphrase this passage.

IV, 2.

1. What theory of monarchical government underlies 1–30?
2. What is indicated in 62b–65 regarding the private or public nature of the war? Is this condition peculiar to this war, or even to the Middle Ages?
3. What is the nature of the irony in 75b–76? Would it have been lost upon Shakespeare's audience?
4. With 79–80 compare IV, 1, 183–184.
5. Note the passivity of the rebels when they learn of Lancaster's treachery. Do you think the poet should have given one of them a long speech of indignant protest, thereby showing the audience how to feel at this juncture?
6. What is the effect upon your feeling toward Prince Hal of this act of his younger brother? Which of the two sons is more like his father?

IV, 3.

1. What evidence as to courage or cowardice in 1–19? Explain 20–22. Paraphrase 33–35.
2. Does it seem natural that Falstaff should quote from

Cæsar's *Commentaries*? Compare II, 2, 134–137. But note that the " thrasonical brag " of " *Veni, vidi, vici* " must have been widely known even among those who could not read their mother tongue. What attitude toward Julius Cæsar is shown here? Is it seen also in Shakespeare's play of the name ? Can you explain it on semi-patriotic grounds ?

3. What phrase of extraordinary beauty in 49–61 ? What qualities of a poet does Falstaff possess and what does he utterly lack ?

4. Is Falstaff anxious to be believed? See 74–76. Compare this entire episode with *Part I*, V, 4, 111 *ff.*

5. What is Falstaff's manner toward Lancaster? Is it as successful as usual? Why? Does this scene give you any new insight into the reasons for Falstaff's cultivation of Hal's society? With 90–91 compare *Part I*, V, 4, 161–162. Compare the two brothers.

6. Is there any truth in 92–93a ? Or is this mere egotism ? What evidence that Falstaff's pride is hurt? With 93b–96 compare II, 2, 7b–13a.

7. Falstaff's derivation of all the heroic virtues from sherris-sack is largely whimsical. Setting this aside, how much truth do you find in his fundamental thesis that " Never none of these demure, sober-blooded boys who love not men like Falstaff and whom one cannot make laugh, come to any good " ? How does all this bear upon your estimate of Hal?

8. Falstaff's genius is founded solidly, like all true genius, upon common sense. His common sense has not been duly recognized because it is so overwrought by the arabesque leafage of his wit. Try to trace it through this greatest and most famous of his soliloquies. Do you find any wisdom whatever in his prescription of the use of wine to such " demure boys " as Prince John ? If possible, compare his theories on this subject with those of the Falstaff of modern English literature — G. K. Chesterton — as expressed in *Orthodoxy*.

9. Several passages of Shakespeare, torn from their context, have been so widely quoted as to create a popular

impression that the poet was in favor of total abstinence. After reading this soliloquy, manifestly written *con amore*, what is your opinion on the point? Compare *Othello*, II, 3, 280–316.

IV, 4.

1. With l. 54 compare sonnet 70. How do you think Shakespeare learned this great truth? How does the line bear upon the differences between Hal and Prince John?
2. Comment fully upon l. 55.
3. Note that in 54–66 the king repeats the same forebodings which Hal successfully combated in *Part I*, III, 2, and in his later actions. Why does the king return to his fears?
4. Do 67–78 explain Hal's mode of life? Is the explanation morally and logically sound?

IV, 5.

1. Do you find Hal's action in taking up the crown and then leaving the room both natural and convincing? Argue for or against.
2. By what means does Hal quiet his father? Compare *I Henry IV*, III, 2.
3. What preparation in 213b–216?

V, 1.

1. What is revealed in this scene regarding Falstaff's attitude toward the prince? What pathos and irony in this?
2. What scenes are linked by this scene?

V, 2.

1. Dramatic purpose of the foreboding speeches of the Chief Justice and those about him?
2. In what connection have we heard before of the incident mentioned in 70–71?
3. Explain 89–90 in the light of previous events.
4. We have been told many times that Hal proposes to

change his mode of life. Are the events of this scene well chosen to show that he has so changed ? Why?

V, 3.

1. How does Master Silence illustrate in this scene the truth of IV, 3, 92 *ff.* ? Does he seem consistent with his name and with his character as previously shown? Are we to accept the beautiful phrase, " Now comes in the sweet of the night," as original with him? With 52b–53a compare II, 4, 396–397.

2. Compare the "humor" of Pistol with that of Silence Are these two characters "humors" in the strict Jonsonian sense? Compare the date of this play with that of Jonson's *Every Man in his Humour*, in which Shakespeare acted. Note that Pistol and Silence are seen for the first time in *Part II*. Note also that Silence is mentioned in Jonson's *Every Man out of his Humour*, V, 2, acted by Shakespeare's company in 1599. What inference ?

3. Enumerate the character contrasts in this scene.

4. Would the scene have been more or less effective than it is here if placed before rather than after V, 2 ? How does its actual position increase the irony in 128–145 ? How does it lessen our shock of surprise and pity in V, 5, 51 *ff.* ?

V, 4.

1. What previous scene does this recall? Can you explain why Doll and the Hostess select just this special peculiarity of the beadle's for abuse, in 20–34?

2. What is the value of this scene in the way of preparation ?

V, 5.

1. What is the artistic and moral necessity of the "rejection of Falstaff"? How has the poet prepared for this by presenting the more corrupt and less engaging phases of Falstaff's character in recent scenes? What special preparation in V, 3 ?

2. Should the part of Falstaff be acted here in such a way as to show a broken heart, a mind that has denied moral issues upon which the moral issue is suddenly forced, sudden realization of a misspent life, or merely the disappointment of an adventurer and a heartless parasite? There are few passages in Shakespeare that offer greater opportunities to the actor. Note that this acting must be done, for the most part, in a pause between l. 75 and l. 76. Did Hal order the imprisonment of Falstaff?

HENRY V

GENERAL QUESTIONS

1. Does the poet gain more than he loses in sacrificing the great character of Falstaff in this play? Why does he do so? If Falstaff had been retained, would he cut the same figure as in the Henry IV plays? According to Holinshed, Sir John Fastolfe was left by Exeter as his lieutenant at Harfleur. Recalling the popular identifications of Shakespeare's Falstaff with Sir John Oldcastle and with Sir John Fastolfe, together with the indignation of the descendants of these worthies, can you explain the report of Falstaff's death?

2. Note that the war is occasioned by the clash of personal interests, and that our attention is held to the fortunes of individuals. How much of this is due to the necessities of stage presentation and in how far may it be regarded as a correct representation of warfare in the late Middle Ages?

3. Outline broadly the various modes of appeal to English patriotism in this play.

*4. Comment fully upon Prologue to Act I, 15–31a. What evidence is there here that the poet was well aware of the criticisms brought against the English chronicle-play technic in such works as Sir Philip Sidney's *Defence of Poesy* and implied in the "classic" or "regular" plays of the schools as well as in the dramas of Jonson? How will the play foreshadowed in these lines differ from a Greek or Roman tragedy or from a play by Racine or Corneille?

5. Why was Shakespeare's technic so little affected by the arguments of men much more learned than he pretended to be? What means is proposed by the Chorus by which the audience may partially offset the imperfections of the chronicle method?

6. Does the dramatic or the epic interest predominate in this play ? Compare the two plays on Henry IV in this respect. Can you explain the slight difference on the ground of differences in the characters of the two kings presented ?

7. Study the alternation of serious and comic scenes throughout the play. By what means are these two sorts of material linked together ? Is this linking more or less successful than in the Henry IV plays ? Why ? Do you find that the serious action is less interesting, on the whole, than the comic, as was the case in the earlier plays ? If there is a difference in this respect, try to explain it.

8. Like most very great artists, Shakespeare admired men of action. Henry V is commonly called his " ideal man of action." But can you give reasons why he must not be called his " ideal man " ? Compare question 3 on I, 2.

9. Cite several instances each of economy in time, in place, in incident, and in character. A good example of the latter is to be found in the theft by Bardolph of the pax, a theft which Holinshed attributes to " a soldier." Where and why does the poet add characters and incidents to the account as it came to him ? This has to do, mainly, with the subplot.

DETAILED QUESTIONS

PROLOGUE

1. What several purposes are served by this prologue ? Does it lead you to expect a play in which the epic or the dramatic element will predominate ?

2. In 8b–27, what is implied as to the sort of effect that Shakespeare tried to produce in his plays ? Realistic or symbolic in stage-craft ? Compare the effects sought on the modern stage.

*3. Give two reasons why the poet is somewhat more sensitive than usual to the classical lines of criticism — one of the reasons having to do with the peculiar nature of his material in this play and the other with the technical ideas of his fellow dramatists which were being stressed at about the time the play was produced.

I, 1.

1. How does this scene bridge the gap between the Prince Hal of the two Henry IV plays and the king of this play? With whom did the idea of the French war originate? Why is the poet so careful to make this clear?

I, 2.

1. How do Henry's two objections to engaging in the French war do him credit?

2. The motives that actuate the churchmen to incite Henry to war are, according to modern standards, morally base. Do you think the man who could speak 21–28 should have been able to see this? How does the poet show historical insight in making Henry so largely dependent upon the advice of his clergy?

3. Does Shakespeare wish to interpret Henry's French campaign as a sort of holy war? Why? How does he show Henry in this scene as something more than a mere soldier king? Does Henry see deeply into moral issues? Does his character seem the product of inner struggle or of outer action?

4. What is gained for the character of Henry by postponing the entrance of the ambassadors and their insulting message until after the interview with the two churchmen?

5. As a matter of history, it is well known that Henry purchased the support of the church by his infamous religious persecutions. How does the poet warp these facts to his dramatic purpose?

6. Criticize the style of this and of the preceding scene, especially as to length of speeches. See 183–220.

II, Prologue

1. How do these lines, like those of the first prologue, exhibit an acknowledgment of dramaturgic principles unusual in Shakespeare's plays ? Would you attribute this to a recent and heated all-night controversy with Ben Jonson over the wine-cups at the Mermaid, or simply to the fact that in this play, for the first time in his chronicle writing since his work on *III Henry VI*, Shakespeare is obliged to set much of his action outside of England ? Do you see any possible connection between all of this and the fact that *Henry V* is the last chronicle play that Shakespeare wrote alone ? He had learned his art, especially as to tragedy, in writing chronicles. Does he seem, in this play, to have outgrown the form ?

II, 1.

1. Note the similarities and contrasts between Pistol and Nym. How does the action of Bardolph show up their essential similarity ?

2. How does this scene connect the present play with *II Henry IV*? What other purposes does it serve ? How is it related to the main action ?

II, 2.

1. Is the effect of 66–181 enhanced or weakened by the previous disclosure in 1–11 and in the Prologue to Act II ? How do 39–60 increase the effect of the scene ?

2. In Henry's unduly long and passionate speech, 94–142, does the extensive comment upon the traitor's past life and his relations to Henry advance the action or reflect character ? What is the purpose of this speech ? To show that just before the great deeds of his mature manhood Henry definitely cut himself loose from his "wilder days" ? Or may we interpret the lyric intensity of this passage as arising from the poet's own sense of injustice in the faithlessness of one of his own friends — such as is vaguely indicated in sonnets 82–96 ? Some

critics who are worthy of a careful hearing think that
Shakespeare often wrote of his own private life and
emotions under cover of his *dramatis personæ*. Hazlitt,
for example, thinks that in his treatment of the refor-
mation of Hal the poet was treating, in a broad and
general way, experiences of his own.

II, 3.

1. Discuss fully the elements of pathos in this scene. Note
   that almost the only touches of nobility that we ever see
   in those present in this scene are due to the influence
   of the ignoble man who lies dead within.

2. Although Theobald's wonderfully fortunate guess,
   " And 'a babbled of green fields," shines in the memory
   forever and has beauty enough almost to reconcile the
   poet's ghost to the two centuries of Shakespearean
   criticism, do you think it in harmony with Falstaff's
   character? Or is there a peculiar beauty in the idea
   that after fifty, " or by 'r Lady, inclining to three-score,"
   years of addiction to sack-and-sugar and kindred frail-
   ties, he should go away " and it had been any christom
   child " ?

II, 4.

1. In what ways is this scene designed to excite the patriotic fervor of the audience? How does it increase
   admiration for Henry?

2. What character contrasts are presented?

III, Prologue

1. In the Prologue to Act I the poet has done little more
   than ask that the audience compensate in imagination
   for the inadequacies of his stage presentation. What
   does he do, over and above this, in the present prologue?
   What influence had the poverty of Shakespeare's stage
   in scenic effects upon his art? How does this prologue
   abridge the action? Compare the first prologue, 28-32.

III, 1.

1. Comment upon the lack of realism in this scene, a long speech spoken in the midst of battle. Explain it with reference to Elizabethan taste and staging.
2. What are the merits of this speech to soldiers before battle? How does it increase our sense of the richness of Henry's mind?

III, 2.

1. Where have we heard before the sort of sentiment expressed in 12–14 and where has the boy acquired his philosophy? Also, where has he contracted the habit of soliloquy?
2. What peculiarities of the Irish, Scotch, and Welsh, respectively, are presented in 61 *ff.*? Does the dialect seem good in each case? Comment fully. What significance do you find in the fact that representatives of the three Celtic peoples, always troublesome to English kings, are here employed as officers in Henry's army?

III, 4.

1. Farmer did not think Shakespeare wrote this scene or even authorized it. Give reasons for or against this opinion. Note that it preserves the alternation of serious and comic scenes, that it gives a glimpse of Henry's future queen before she appears in Act V, that it shows her taking the lessons in English of which she will stand sorely in need, and, finally, that it allows some time for the passage of Henry's army from Harfleur to beyond the River Somme. Compare III, 5, 1.
2. What would be the effect of such a scene upon Shakespeare's audience — especially of Katherine's feeling that such English words as "foot" and "gown" "*sont mots de son mauvais, corruptible, gros, et impudique*"? How much of Katherine's French was probably understood? How is it cleverly arranged so that the meaning may be conveyed largely by gestures?

III, 5.

1. What is the purpose or value in the French king's calling over of the names of his vassals in 40 *ff.* ? Why is so much made of the sickness and famine in Henry's army?

III, 6.

1. How has the pedantic Fluellen been deceived by Pistol?

2. How does Henry throw all prudence to the winds, or, rather, Shakespeare all considerations of probability, in 148 *ff.*? Note 152–153. Are not " craft and vantage " essential to all warfare, civilized or savage? How do you characterize the English idea of warfare, as represented by Henry and Shakespeare's audience? For, of course, the poet is here giving his public what it wants.

3. Point out several respects in which these preparations for battle differ in spirit and method from what one would expect in modern warfare. Note the lack of secrecy, the personal animosity and insults, the conditions of the duel and the idea of trial by battle.

4. Note and explain the variations between prose and verse in the last two scenes.

III, 7.

1. How does the boasting in this scene contrast with that of Henry in the preceding scene? Does it show egotism or extreme self-confidence? What is the poet's purpose in this contrast?

2. What features of this scene are overdrawn and calculated to " make the unskillful laugh and the judicious grieve "? Does Shakespeare seem to feel, here, that the censure of one judicious person should " outweigh a whole theater of others"? Why?

3. How does the Dauphin contrast with Henry? With this scene compare III, 5, 64–66.

IV, 1.

1. Comment upon 126–139 in the light of modern ideas. Did Shakespeare see the weakness in Bates's second speech? Did he expect his audience to see it?

2. How do 136–139 and 140–153 throw all the dramatic interest of the situation upon Henry, thereby justifying, in appearance at least, the treatment of the battle as a purely personal matter? We know that Henry is not alone in danger and that many men are to die. But the dramatic method necessitates the treatment of great mass interests in terms of personal, individual interests. This is one reason why Shakespeare has been charged with aristocratic, anti-social prejudices. Can you detect in this scene an effort to compensate for this defect of the dramatic mode?

3. Which party has the better of the argument in 87–241? Does Henry's reply to Williams in 154–196 seem cogent and satisfying? Why? Was it intended by the poet to be so? Compare 247 *ff*.

4. What examples of dramatic irony in 87–241? How does Henry's earlier training stand him in good stead here?

5. What is the purpose and effect of 242–301? Compare this soliloquy with a similar passage in *II Henry IV*, especially as to poetic beauty and intensity.

6. Comment fully upon 306–322.

7. The poet has been at pains in this play to show that Henry, although England's greatest soldier king, is no mere Hotspur, living in and for battle. What has been done to show this before the present scene? What is done in this scene?

8. Point out passages in the scene in which Henry is troubled by doubts, fears, self-pity, the burden of others' woes, the sense of inherited guilt. Should a really heroic man be aware of these things or know what fear is? Does all this tend to lower the king in your estimation and to give an impression of weakness? Note that just at the time when Henry feels the whole crushing weight

of his responsibilities, he is called upon to strengthen others. What is the relation of this scene to III, 7 ?

9. How does the effect of this scene compare with that made by Henry's speeches in III, 6, 148 *ff.*? Can you reconcile the difference?

10. Explain variations between prose and verse in this scene.

IV, 2.

1. What is the purpose of this scene? What earlier scene does it resemble?

IV, 3.

1. With 20–28 compare *I Henry IV*, I, 3, 206–208, and V, 4, 147–162. Explain the apparent contradiction.

2. What merits do you find in Henry's famous speech, 18–67? Where do you see the Prince Hal of earlier days in these lines?

3. What is the relation of this scene to the preceding and to IV, 1? How is the effect of Henry's heroism in this scene enhanced by IV, 1?

IV, 4.

1. With l. 39 compare II, 1, 75, and with l. 68 compare II, 3, 58.

2. What is the effect intended in this capture of a French "gentleman of good family" by such a person as Pistol?

IV, 5.

1. Coleridge thought he saw a good excuse for these "introductory scraps of French instantly followed by good nervous Mother-English." Do you see any excuse?

IV, 6.

1. What artistic and dramatic fault do you find in the unhistorical material dealing with the death of York, and especially with the part that refers to his love for Suffolk?

2. Discuss fully Henry's order to kill the prisoners and Shakespeare's method of treating it.

IV, 7.

1. How does Fluellen's talk about Alexander serve to soften the effect of the incident touched upon at the end of scene 6? What earlier instances of Fluellen's pedantry and fondness for antiquarian parallels? How does the environment enhance the humorous effect of this?
2. With l. 66 compare 9b–11a and IV, 6, 37–38.
3. Do you think 116–120 true to Fluellen's character as previously presented? For what purpose is he suddenly made ridiculous, almost foolish, in this speech?
4. Why did the poet introduce the incident of the glove? Does it harmonize well with the battle scenes? Is the incident in keeping with Henry's character? Note that Henry details two of the greatest lords of his kingdom, one of them his brother, to oversee a quarrel which he has instigated between a hot-headed Welsh pedant and a common soldier. What is the propriety or significance of this? How is it related to incidents of the Henry IV plays and to IV, 1, 253 ff.? Compare V, 2, 126b–130.

IV, 8.

1. What preparation has been given for the piety shown in l. 111? How does this contrast with Henry's manner of life in the earlier plays?
2. As an illustration of the differences between history and the history-play, note that 130–131 give an impression of victory, whereas Henry's first French campaign failed utterly in its real purpose. After the brilliant victory at Agincourt, Henry was obliged to hasten home with a starving, disease-ridden army.

V, Prologue

1. What is accomplished by this prologue that could not have been accomplished by more legitimate dramatic methods?

V, 1.

1. Has Fluellen been consistently handled? Note 78–81a, and compare the treatment of him in IV, 7. What are the elements of his character?

2. In Pistol we see the last flicker of the more ignoble phases of the dead Falstaff's spirit. Bardolph and Nym have been hanged. Mistress Quickly is dead. Why does the poet reserve the final disgrace of the weakest and worst of the group until the day of Henry's greatest glory?

3. Explain why Pistol speaks in verse while all the other inferior characters are content with prose.

V, 2.

1. Criticize the style and thought of 23–67. What qualities of this speech may have been intended as characteristic of the French? How does the speech contrast with those of Henry?

2. Explain Henry's use of prose in his wooing of Katherine. What is there in his manner that Shakespeare's audience would recognize with pride as characteristically English? Since Katherine was to be an English queen, she could not be used as a foil for Henry's admirable qualities. What character is so used here?

3. Compare this wooing-scene with that in *I Henry IV*, III, 1.

4. Was there danger that the present scene might destroy the play's unity of tone and the consistency of Henry's character? Has the poet avoided this danger? How?

ROMEO AND JULIET

GENERAL QUESTIONS

1. Outline the plot. What is the initial incident? Where is the climax of the action? Outline the time scheme of the play. How is this headlong haste worked out in the characters as well as in the action?

2. Collect several passages of unmistakably early work. Place beside these certain other passages of work far more nearly mature in thought, feeling, expression, and versification. Define carefully the differences between the two kinds. How do you explain the presence of the two types of work in the same play?

3. Does the source of the tragedy seem to lie primarily in the characters, in the family feud, or in adverse fate? Show that it lies to some extent in each of these but choose the most important source.

4. Write a careful estimate of Romeo. Do you consider the treatment of his love for Rosaline a blemish upon the play? Explain carefully the function of this material. What tragic fault do you find in his character? Discuss the powers of his mind as those of a lyric poet. What evidence that the dramatist thought of him as a lyric poet?

5. How much is made of the family feud? Why? Does this seem good tragic material? By what means is it converted into terms of personality — the only terms in which the dramatist can present the abstract?

*6. Collect the instances of tragic accident. How much place should accident have in determining the events of modern tragedy? Why different in ancient tragedy? In comedy? Does it seem to be given more or less importance and prominence here than in other Shakespearean tragedies with which you are familiar?

Does this difference seem due to differences in characters and in purpose?

7. Is the poet trying, in this play, as in his later tragedies, to present the tragedy of a powerful individual ruined by the warring forces of his own nature, or is he treating, in a more generalized way, the tragedy of youthful passion everywhere, in all time? In what sense is Romeo a tragic hero?

8. There is no mercy in Shakespeare's tragic world for one-sided, overbalanced men. The counsel of perfection is as imperative here as in the remorseless world of nature. Only the trifler can safely be one-sided. The strong man, like a tall tower, must be strong at all points or be torn in pieces by his own strength. What lack of balance do you find in Romeo? What excess? What blindness to fact? Show that these things are closely related to his best qualities.

9. Discuss the character of Juliet as to strength, delicacy, modesty, intelligence. What qualities of her nature seem merely the feminine counterpart of those of Romeo? In what respects is she the superior of her lover?

*10. Discuss the function of Mercutio in the play. Study the character and psychology of the Nurse. Compare her with Mistress Quickly in *II Henry IV*.

11. Does the play leave you with a feeling, akin to despair, that these two beautiful souls, trusting themselves impetuously and whole-heartedly to the most inevitable law of nature and to their own highest instincts, have been ruined and crushed through a monstrous injustice? Or does the peace restored between the two families seem adequate to the price they paid? Is this latter interpretation the one the poet would have us accept? But we have loved this boy and this girl. How much do we care about the petty brawls of their families, after they are gone? Where does Mercutio express this? Does there seem to be a fault here? From Æschylus to Joseph Conrad, high tragedy has ever been raising the insoluble problems, keeping us aware that we live in an unintelligible

world. In his first essay at tragedy, does Shakespeare
succeed in giving this effect?

DETAILED QUESTIONS

I, 1.

1. In what fixed form of verse is the prologue written?
   Compare I, 5, 94–108, and the Prologue to Act II. Is
   there any indication in the form and style of these
   passages as to the date at which they were written?
   Do you think they are in good taste? Is there any way
   in which they fit the spirit of the play?

2. Is the purpose of the prologue expository or dramatic?
   Compare it with the Prologue to *Troilus and Cressida*
   or with any of those in *Henry V*. Do you find that
   some "moral" of the play is indicated here? If so,
   what is it? Is it a confession of weakness that the poet
   should have to tell us what the play means?

3. Distinguish Samson and Gregory. Are they consistently
   drawn or is their wit sometimes too good to suit their
   condition in life?

4. Mood and mental state of Romeo as presented in 125–
   161? Why is this given here, before Romeo's entrance?

5. Comment upon 157–159 in the light of the entire play.

6. Elements in the description of Romeo's passion that
   mark it as boyish and immature or as manly and real?

7. Discuss 177–189. What is the nature of Romeo's talk
   about his love?

8. The prologue has indicated the existence of a feud between the two houses. Why, then, is a street fight between them presented in the scene immediately following? Is the sympathy of the audience to be enlisted
   for or against the feud? Why?

9. Character of the Prince? For what later scene or incident is his present severity a preparation?

10. Into what three divisions does the scene fall? In what
    order are the characters presented? Explain the pur-
    pose of this order. Why is Tybalt presented here?

11. This scene, although so full of stirring bustle, is really almost pure exposition. As such, it is one of the best that the poet ever wrote. Point out some of its excellences.

I, 2.

1. Purpose of the first five lines?
*2. What is Juliet's age in Brooke's poem? Why changed by Shakespeare? An ancient church statute placed the age at which a girl might marry without her parents' consent at fifteen years. What is Romeo's age?
3. Character of Capulet as shown here.
4. Show that the main action of the play begins with l. 57.
5. Does the list of guests read strangely? Does it scan? Comment.
6. What is accomplished by way of exposition in this scene?

I, 3.

1. Discuss the character of the Nurse. Is she a type or an individual? Do you think she was studied from the life or imagined?
2. Is any purpose of contrast served in the character of the Nurse? Contrast of what nature and with whom?
3. Judging from 72-74, what is the age of Lady Capulet? From I, 5, 34-36, estimate the age of Old Capulet. Why is the poet so careful to give these apparently insignificant details? What bearing have they upon the position of Juliet?
4. Outline and criticize the metaphor of the book, 81-88. Compare *The Rape of Lucrece*, 99-103.
5. Note the length of Juliet's speeches in this scene and compare with those of the Nurse. Indication regarding character? Position of Juliet in her family? How does her family regard her? What elements of pathos do you find in her position?
6. How does this scene advance the exposition? How linked to the preceding and to the following scene?

I, 4.

1. Dramatic value of Romeo's hesitation in going to the ball?
2. Character of Mercutio? How does his name fit him? With what character does he contrast?
3. Comment upon the long Queen Mab speech, 53–94. Does it advance the action or have any bearing upon it? Does it give us a clearer notion of any character except that of the speaker? Is it dramatic? Is it lyric? Is it in harmony with the tone of the play?
4. Imagine this speech as spoken on the stage. Group the other characters about the speaker. Remember that the company is on its way to a ball. Would this be considered good dramatic writing to-day? What different standards of taste and different public demands upon the theater made it permissible on Shakespeare's stage?
5. What two scenes does this scene link together? How does it assist in exposition?

I, 5.

1. Purpose of the bustling action of servants and of the conversation between the two Capulets? What earlier bits of action and conversation have had the same purpose?
2. Has Romeo's love at first sight been prepared for adequately? How? How does he express himself about this new love? Compare his speeches in I, 1.
3. How has Juliet's sudden love for Romeo been prepared for?
4. What dramatic and æsthetic purpose is served by sounding the jarring notes of Tybalt's anger just after the lyric solo in which Romeo sings his new-found love?
5. Discuss the character of Tybalt. Why is it made so thin and repellent? Compare II, 4, 18–19, and III, 1, 80 and 104. What is Tybalt's sole function in the play? Why and how are we here allowed to sympathize with him for a moment?

6. Does Romeo act in this scene like a mature and experienced man under the circumstances? Do we excuse his inconstancy to Rosaline? Why and how is this made easy? What is the nature of this second love, as shown here, in comparison with the first?

7. What notes of foreboding are struck in this scene? Is it a scene primarily of exposition or of real action?

8. This is the first of the five scenes in which Romeo and Juliet appear together. What is its general character, mood, or tone, taken as a whole?

II, 1.

*1. Outline the stage setting for this scene. See G. P. Baker's *Development of Shakespeare as a Dramatist*, p. 69 *ff.*

2. Æsthetic and technical purposes of this scene?

II, 2.

1. Remembering that the scenes of this play were marked by editors — in this case by Rowe — do you think a division is wisely made here?

*2. Outline the stage setting of this scene. See frontispiece to Albright's *The Shakespearean Stage* and the drawing of the Swan Theater facing p. 210 of Baker's *Development of Shakespeare.*

3. Follow the movements of Juliet during Romeo's speech, 2–25.

4. Beginning with this speech and continuing through the scene, what changes in the manner of phrasing do you notice?

5. Mood of Romeo in this scene? Compare Juliet. Which dominates the other? Which seems the stronger? Which sees more clearly the difficulties of their situation? Compare Ruskin's *Sesame and Lilies*, paragraphs 56–58, in the chapter "Of Queens' Gardens." Which of the lovers is the center of interest here? How made so and why?

6. Why does not Romeo show more surprise when he learns of Juliet's love?

7. Compare Juliet's attitude and manner toward her lover with that shown this same day toward her mother. Compare especially the length of her speeches. Has the poet shielded Juliet from the charge of boldness? If so, by what means?

8. In Brooke's poem, weeks elapse between the first and the second meetings of the lovers. How long here? Why is it dramatically necessary that Juliet should be thus precipitate? How is it made to seem reasonable that she should be? In what passage does the poet present an apology for her?

9. Dramatic value of the Nurse's interruptions? Compare the last lines of I, 3, and I, 5.

II, 3.

1. Character of Friar Laurence? How does his occupation here serve as preparation for later events? Note the moralizing nature of his first speeches.

2. What is the value for the play of 1–30? How does it contrast in mood with the preceding scene? Why is so much made, in this speech, of the opposing forces of good and evil in plants and men?

3. A "chorus character" is one that serves as a norm by which those about him may be measured. He often expresses the dramatist's own judgment upon the people and action of the piece. Does the term fit Friar Laurence?

4. What is the application to the entire play of 17–22? Compare II, 6, 9–15.

II, 4.

1. Value of 19–27 and of Mercutio's dislike for the art of fencing? How does this passage link I, 5, with III, 1?

2. How does the mood of Romeo contrast with that in which we last saw him? Why? Why is Romeo made to outdo even Mercutio, the arch-jester, at his own game?

3. By how much does this scene advance the plot? Into what divisions does it fall? What scenes are linked by the material of the last division?

II, 5.

1. What is accomplished by this scene? To what elements does it owe its charm?

II, 6.

1. Comment upon the Friar's opening words. In what mood are they answered? Try to describe fully the state of mind in which Romeo speaks.
2. What underlying meaning do you see in 16b–17?
3. This is the third meeting of the lovers. What stage of the main story does it mark? What is the prevailing mood of the scene? By what contrasting mood is it colored?

III, 1.

1. What is the dramatic purpose and irony in 16–33? Note that the immediate cause of Mercutio's fight with Tybalt is a mere pun, a quibble, which he makes himself, in order to become the aggressor. Does he accuse Benvolio of any such extravagance as this? Is it appropriate that Mercutio should die, so to speak, of a pun?
2. What new light on Mercutio's character is given in his words just before he is borne away? What is the value for the play of the last words we hear from him?
3. What necessity of the Elizabethan stage is recalled by l. 110?
4. Give several reasons why the poet found it advisable to have Mercutio killed early in the play. Show that his death was dramatically necessary.
5. What new elements of Romeo's character are shown in 114–136?
6. By what means is Romeo relieved of blame for the death of Tybalt? Why was this necessary? If you felt it necessary to blame him for this act, how would your feeling toward the entire play be affected?
7. Does Benvolio report the details of the quarrel exactly? Why?

8. Character of Lady Capulet as shown in her two speeches in this scene? What is this preparation for? Is she one of those women who place family feeling in the seat of reason and think with their prejudices? Who is the most hateful person in the play, now that Tybalt is no more?

9. Define carefully your feeling for Romeo at the close of this scene.

10. Name several different lines of preparation for the events of this scene.

11. How does this scene advance the action and what part does it play in the entire plot? Where is the climax of the play?

III, 2.

1. What features of Juliet's speech, 1–31, mark it as lyrical rather than dramatic? Can you justify the presence of a lyrical passage here? What other purely lyrical passages do you remember, from this play? Compare III, 5, 1–35.

2. Criticize 36–68. Show that this passage would make very heavy demands upon the actress. Do you think it was written early in Shakespeare's career, or later? Why? What preparation do you find in 45–60? How does this consideration help the entire passage?

3. Explain Juliet's outcry upon her lover for the killing of Tybalt. Had Tybalt been dear to her? Is there a touch of heredity here? How long is it since she would herself have looked upon Romeo as a foe and have spoken much as her mother has spoken?

4. Where have we had expressions similar to those in 73–84 earlier in the play?

5. What do 97–127 indicate regarding Juliet's attitude toward her father and mother? How do these lines intensify the effect of her utter loneliness?

6. What new revelations of Juliet's character are made in this scene? What is the purpose of the scene?

III, 3.

1. What important element of Romeo's character is shown by his manner in receiving the Friar's announcement?
2. Is the extravagance of 29–51 the language of real passion or merely the conventional rant of the Elizabethan stage? Do you find single lines that are exceptions to your statement?
3. With l. 98 compare III, 4, 8 and III, 2, 45–50. Comment.
4. Do you think 108–158 a justifiable criticism of Romeo's general character and present mood? What is the dramatic value of this passage?

III, 5.

1. Point out the elements of pathos, dramatic irony, and foreshadowing in 43–64.
2. Nature of the consolation Lady Capulet offers in 70–74? What double purpose does this serve? How does it serve at once as characterization and as an illustration of Juliet's loneliness?
3. Discuss Juliet's evasive replies to her mother in 82–103. What is their moral aspect, if any? What sort of pleasure would the audience take in this passage?
4. With l. 141 compare 202–205. Comment.
5. Discuss 214–227. Show that this advice is or is not consistent with the character of the speaker as previously presented. What is its effect upon Juliet? How does it affect our sympathy for her? What other passages have had a similar effect? Compare especially 210–212.
6. Outline the preparation that has been given for Old Capulet's harshness. What seems to be the poet's opinions on the subject of parental authority? What do you think of Juliet's rejection of that authority? Compare 204–205.
7. By what successive steps has Juliet been rushed out of girlhood into maturity?
8. Point out some of the elements of pathos in her present condition.

IV, 1.

1. Comment upon the form and manner of 18-38. What is Juliet's mood as she keeps up her part in this highly artificial dialogue? Compare 44-45.

2. Compare Juliet's speeches in 44-126 with those to her mother in III, 5.

3. What comment seems appropriate upon l. 42? Upon 81-85?

4. What suggests to the Friar the plan outlined in 89-120? In what sense is this plan the germ idea of the entire play?

5. For what later scenes does this scene prepare?

IV, 2.

1. With l. 2 compare III, 4, 23-28. What subtle characterization do you find here? What do such apparently trifling but really important matters as this indicate regarding the advantages to be gained in careful and close study of the poet? What do they indicate regarding the care with which the poet worked over his material?

2. How is the outcome of the plot profoundly affected by the change made by Old Capulet in the date set for the wedding? Does Juliet realize this? Is this arbitrary change characteristic of Old Capulet?

3. Is it artistically justifiable to base so much upon so slight and accidental a circumstance? Is it "true to life"? Explain the repetition of the announcement of the changed date in 33-40?

IV, 3.

1. What is implied in line 5? Considering that the Nurse makes no reply, can you see the reason why Shakespeare makes her false to Romeo in an earlier scene? What does the Nurse expect Juliet to do?

2. Follow closely the emotional progress of the speaker in 15-58. Discuss the power of imagination shown here. What does Juliet chiefly fear in the step she is about to take? Are her fears physical or spiritual? Is this

normal and right? What finally overcomes her personal
fears? Do you think this famous and wonderful passage
is entirely satisfactory, natural, convincing, or has it a
theatrical air of unreality?

3. Describe the stage setting of this scene.

IV, 4.

1. How was this scene staged? Purpose of the comic material? What time elapses during the scene?

IV, 5.

1. Comment upon the rant of 34–64. How does it compare in purpose with that of III, 3, 29–51?

2. By what means is the mourning for Juliet made merely
conventional, hollow, and unconvincing? Is this in harmony with the characters of the mourners as we know
them? Why is this done? Why would it have been a
serious error to have made this mourning very solemn
and affecting?

3. Has the order in which the characters appear any relation to the respective degrees of their sorrow? Do we
really pity any one?

4. Explain carefully the dramatic purpose of 96–150.

V, 1.

1. Value of Romeo's elation, 1–11? Compare l. 24.

*2. What change in Romeo's character is indicated or fore-
told in his reception of the news? Is his present action
and manner consistent with his character as we know it?

*3. Explain the psychology of 39–48. Compare D. G.
Rossetti's poem, *The Woodspurge.* Explain 80–83 and
their fitness to the occasion.

V, 2.

*1. What are the consequences of the accident indicated in
8–16? See Dowden's discussion of this point in *Shakespeare, His Mind and Art.*

2. Purpose of this scene? Why is it not made interesting in and for itself?

V, 3.

1. What is the dramatic value of Paris's fear of being seen? What light does it throw upon his character?

2. What is the mood of Romeo as indicated in 22–39?

3. The killing of Paris is an incident of the poet's own invention. Does it add to the effect of the scene more than it detracts? Apart from this consideration, is there any reason why Paris should die at the hand of Romeo? Does Romeo act like a master of himself and of events in this scene with Paris?

4. Compare 88–120 with IV, 3, 14–58, for emotional range, poetic intensity, and character portrayal.

5. Comment in some detail upon the change and growth in Romeo since his appearance in Act I, as indicated in this scene.

6. Some critics think the poet missed a great opportunity for an effective and pathetic scene in allowing Romeo to die before Juliet wakes. Imagine the colloquy between the lovers, had Juliet awaked before her lover's death. Would it have been pathetic? Would it have been bearable, if done with an intensity in harmony with the rest of the play?

7. Do Juliet's last words seem adequate? How do they differ from Romeo's? Is this due to differences in character, or to what?

8. With what material and in what mood does the play end? Compare I, 1, and III, 1.

JULIUS CÆSAR

GENERAL QUESTIONS

1. To show the simplicity of the plot material, outline the action in one hundred words or less.

2. Give reasons for the play's comparative poverty in subtle analysis of character and motive and in poetic beauty. What is the influence, in this respect, of the nobly simple, austere, and somewhat stiff personality of Brutus? If Antony had been allowed to dominate and determine the tone of the play, how would the play have differed in effect? It would not be entirely misleading to compare, in this connection, the wonderfully rich and various *Antony and Cleopatra*. *Coriolanus* also has a voluminous majesty and a sumptuous splendor which forbids the assertion that the simplicity of *Julius Cæsar* is due to the poet's estimate of the Roman type of mind.

3. What powers of the poet's mind are scarcely brought into play in this drama? What powers are clearly in evidence?

4. Try to define the exact nature of the pleasure you take in this play. Is it at all like the pleasure you take in any of the great tragedies or in any of the comedies?

5. Why is this play especially suited to the comprehension of children and to the elementary type of mind among adults? (This must not, of course, be understood to imply condemnation, unless we wish to include in that condemnation almost the entire tragic theater of the ancient world.) What scenes do you leave out of consideration in your answers to this and to the three preceding questions?

*6. Would you say that in this play the poet's powers of

expression are in advance of his thought or that they lag behind his thought? Or are thought and expression in a nearly perfect equipoise? Select several passages in illustration. Compare *A Midsummer Night's Dream* and *The Tempest* in this regard.

7. Is the poet preoccupied here with the outer world of action, as in *The Comedy of Errors*, or with the inner world of thought and feeling, as in *Hamlet*? Or do you find in this respect also a healthy balance? What is the bearing of this question upon the character of Brutus?

8. Suggest and support by argument what seems to you a more fitting title for the play.

9. What important character contrasts are presented? What is their purpose or dramatic function?

10. Write out a careful study of the character of Brutus. Try to determine how much the poet sympathized with Brutus and how far he saw beyond him.

11. Discuss fully the treatment of the plebeians. Show that this treatment was necessary in order to provide the proper background for the chief characters. The chief characters are public men. How is their power to be shown? Remember that the tragic drama has always been and perhaps must always be committed to the "great man theory" of Carlyle and to something very like the "superman theory" of Nietzsche.

*12. In spite of the above considerations, does the poet seem to have deepened his shadows unnecessarily in treating the plebs? Is he essentially aristocratic in his social leanings and political thought, as Tolstoy believed? This important question cannot be discussed on the basis of one play alone. *Coriolanus, Romeo and Juliet, II Henry VI*, 4, 10, should be compared. One must not forget the fact that the poet himself came from the very ranks of society which he so often derides. If it can be shown that he was essentially undemocratic in sympathy, then II, 1, 21b–27a, of the present play has a clear application to his own case.

*13. Compare the treatment of the common people in *Rich-*

ard II with that in the present play. Does the poet's scorn of the "great unwashed" go beyond the purely dramatic necessities of the case? Is it not clear, at least, that Shakespeare had no sentimental illusions regarding the coarseness, stupidity, and fickleness of the lower classes, regarding their hatred and fear of all superiority, regarding their astonishing power of selecting for trust and affection the man nearest their own level of mediocrity and vulgarity?

DETAILED QUESTIONS

I, 1.

1. What exposition in this scene? Is it cleverly introduced? What action accompanies it?
2. For what sort of behavior on the part of the populace does this scene prepare? Note especially 37–60. Is the influence of the people in later scenes of sufficient weight to warrant this strong foreshadowing in the first scene? Compare, in this respect, the first scene of *Romeo and Juliet*.

I, 2.

1. What important character trait is marked in l. 24? What hints regarding Antony and Casca do you gather in 1–24?
2. What is the dramatic effect of the soothsayer's words, especially as spoken at just this time?
3. To what passions does Cassius especially appeal in 25–177? Judging from Brutus's character as shown later, does Cassius proceed in just the best possible way? Wherein does he show that his nature is inferior to that of Brutus? What elements in his speeches seem to you particularly artful and telling?
4. Comment upon the masterly touches of characterization in 180–188. Compare 192–195 with 115–118.
5. Discuss the character and mood of the speaker in 192–214. What effect did the poet intend by his stroke of

genius in 213? Compare the character revealed in this
line and in the whole speech with the earlier statements
about Cæsar by Cassius.

6. Does Cæsar speak like an honored citizen in a democracy
or like an absolute potentate? Is Shakespeare intending
to treat Cæsar as a great hero and win for him all possible sympathy? Why?

7. What motive for Cassius's plot against Cæsar is presented here?

8. Explain fully the mood and thought of Brutus in 307–
310.

9. Compare and contrast Brutus, Cassius, Casca, as shown
in this scene.

I, 3.

1. What dramatic effect is intended in the storm and por-
tents of nature? Compare *Macbeth*, II, 4.

2. Is Cassius more or less clever in his treatment of Casca
than in his treatment of Brutus? Why?

3. To what elements of Casca's nature does he appeal
with special force? Would the same appeal have been
effective with Brutus? Note 103–115. Why does he
succeed with Casca so much more easily than with
Brutus?

4. Summarize the exposition of Act I. Summarize the
action. What character dominates the action thus far?

II, 1.

1. Why is the material of 10–34 presented before Cassius
returns to the attack or has made any definite suggestions for future action? How much has Brutus been
dependent upon Cassius's suggestions from the first?
Compare his manner in I, 2.

2. Follow very carefully the movement of thought in 10–
34. Does it show the logic of a man trained in action
or that of an abstract, theoretical, idealistic thinker?
Does Brutus fail, like many another academic spinner
of syllogisms, to bring his logical conclusions to the test
of experience?

3. Cæsar has said that Cassius "thinks too much." What did he mean? Cæsar was himself one of the greatest thinkers, in an important sense of the word, in all history. Would his statement have been at least equally applicable to Brutus? Prove your points by line references.

4. How long a period is spoken of in 61–62? The Feast of Lupercal occurred on February 15.

5. Does Brutus seem more or less conscious of the workings of his own mind than of external events? Compare the state of mind and habit of thought shown in *Macbeth*, I, 7, 1 *ff.*

6. From 53–54, 113–140 and 162–183 infer the motives that have led Brutus into the conspiracy. By what means is the superior power of Brutus shown in 86–228? What is the precise nature of that power? But in what respects is Cassius superior to Brutus? Note also the stiff, Puritanical attitude of 188b–189. Be careful to avoid the general tendency to over-praise Brutus. He should have known how to be honest and dignified without being ungracious and prudish.

7. What dramatic effect is cleverly secured in the references to theatrical performances in 226–227, I, 2, 258–262, and III, 1, 111–116? Compare *Twelfth Night*, III, 4, 140–141 and *Antony and Cleopatra*, V, 2, 216–221.

8. What effect did the poet wish to make by the introduction of Portia? How does it deepen and enrich the characterization of Brutus? Note that with the exception of this and the next two scenes the play deals exclusively with men. With this scene compare *I Henry IV*, II, 3, both as to management and as to outcome.

9. Into what divisions does this scene fall? What character dominates them all? How is the personal power and prestige of Brutus shown at the very end?

II, 2.

1. What is the tone of Cæsar's words in regard to danger and superstition? Do they show real common-sense and fearlessness? Compare 5–6 with 38–43. With 83–90 compare II, 1, 202–211.

2. What finally determines Cæsar to go? What irony is there in this? Does he show himself a hero or a weakling in this scene? Why and how is he made to do so?

3. What fine shades of difference do you find between the relations of husband and wife as shown here and those shown in the preceding scene? How is it significant that the two scenes are set side by side? Does Shakespeare seem to imply that one of the most important things we can know about a man is his attitude toward women and, if he be married, his attitude toward his wife? How do these two men stand this test? The characters of the two women concerned are of course important factors in the case.

III, 1.

1. Discuss the merits of 1–121 as a tableau or stage spectacle. What opportunities would this passage afford a modern stage manager for effective grouping of masses of people? Was Shakespeare's audience interested in this kind of theatrical effect?

2. How is Cæsar made to justify, in a measure, the accusations against him? Make suggestions for the acting of the part of Brutus.

3. Study with care the motives and mood of Antony in 122–253. What have we heard of Antony before he appears? What, especially, is Brutus' estimate of him? What does Cassius think of him? Which of these two is the more likely to be right?

4. What two serious errors in diplomacy are made by Brutus in regard to Antony? Explain how he came to make them?

5. Have Antony's speeches the ring of sincerity? Point out two or three lines of great poetic beauty in these speeches.

III, 2.

1. Discuss the merits of Brutus's speech with special regard to its adaptation to the audience and the occasion. What form and what length of sentence is most em-

ployed? Is the speech readily followed and its main points easily retained? Does it make its chief appeal to the intellect or to the passions? Does the speaker understand passion from his own experience so as to know how to guide and control it in others?

2. Answer each of the above questions with regard to Antony's speeches in 78–257.

3. Comment upon the speeches and actions of the plebeians throughout the scene.

4. To what elements does this scene owe its great effectiveness? Note the simplicity which it has in common with the entire play. Comment upon the use of character contrast.

III, 3.

1. Purpose of this scene? Was it written by an ardent democrat?

IV, 1.

1. What new light is thrown upon Antony's character in 1–40?

2. What is the purpose of the scene?

IV, 3.

1. How was this and the preceding scene staged in Shakespeare's theater?

2. Show that Brutus's error in regard to "better" and "older" is a strong touch of realistic detail, enhancing the illusion of reality.

3. Does Brutus seem fair and just and more in the right than Cassius in 107b–113a? Which of the two bears himself in the more noble and manly fashion throughout the quarrel? Here, as always, a superficial answer may be worse than a wrong one.

4. Is the announcement of Portia's death well timed? Why? How does the manner of the announcement bear upon the character of Brutus? Do you find the manner of the announcement wholly admirable, as well as

the trait of character which it reveals? Is it more or less effective because given so little space?

5. What is Brutus's philosophy, mentioned in l. 145? How has it affected him? In accord with the dictates of his philosophy, Brutus has come to fear a normal expression of normal emotion. Does this make for strength or weakness? Does it really liberate him from the dominion of emotion? Does his sentimental hatred of sentiment make him in any way a braver or better man? Comment fully upon 181–192. Does the upright Brutus prefer an unprovoked lie to a natural tear? Do you think less of Cassius for his perfectly sincere reply in 194–195?

6. What effect is secured in 252–253? What similar effects in the following lines? What is their purpose here?

7. What is the ghost of Cæsar intended to symbolize? Why does not the ghost appear to Cassius also? Compare the similar scene in *Macbeth*.

8. The delineation of Brutus is now complete. He is, on the whole, one of the noblest men and one of the least fitted for this world in all Shakespeare's gallery. How has this powerful scene, which Coleridge said impressed upon him more than any other "the belief of Shakespeare's being superhuman," added to the portrait?

V, 1–4.

1. How do these scenes modify your feeling toward Brutus, if at all? Show that in them he is still regulating his conduct by the "rules of his philosophy" rather than by any spontaneous moral sense of his own and is still somewhat awe-struck before the spectacle of his own nobility.

2. What stage effect was sought by the poet in these scenes? Explain the decided falling-off in dramatic intensity and interest. Was this inevitable and due to the nature of the material? Why would it be less noticeable in acting, especially under Elizabethan conditions?

V, 5.

1. Does the conclusion of the play seem satisfactory in
   all respects? Did the poet bring all his powers to bear
   upon this conclusion? Do you think that, in general,
   Shakespeare was as much interested in *what* happens
   as in *how* and *why* it happens?

MERCHANT OF VENICE

GENERAL QUESTIONS

1. What are the actions or stories of the play? Which are of major and which of minor importance? Into what groups are the characters divided? What character is most important in each group?

2. Which is the main action? Is it the most interesting? Why?

3. What action was probably intended as a foil or contrast to the main action? Does it perfectly fulfill this function?

4. Show in detail by what devices the various actions are interwoven so as to make a harmonious whole.

*5. Write a brief study of the character of Antonio. Is he as interesting as he is admirable? Do you think the poet succeeded as completely in drawing Antonio as in drawing Shylock? Why? Does he seem essentially Italian? Compare and contrast him with his associates. Compare him with the old Roman ideal of manhood represented in Shakespeare's Brutus and with the ideal represented in the moral essays of Seneca, Marcus Aurelius, and Epictetus.

*6. Contrast Shylock with Antonio. Which offers the greater dramatic opportunity? Why? Illustrate your answer by reference to Milton's Satan and God, Tennyson's Lancelot and Arthur, Browning's Guido and Pompilia.

7. Do you think the play is well named? Is Shylock or Antonio the chief and central figure? In what sense? Which is the spring of the action?

*8. What two main phases do you find in the character of Shylock? In which of these does the poet seem quite fair to the Jew? In which does he seem to echo popu-

lar prejudice ? Compare, in this connection, Marlowe's
The Jew of Malta.

9. Shylock counsels prudence, industry, thrift, quiet living. The Italians are boisterous, spendthrift, frivolous.
To which side do your sympathies lean ? How is this
brought about?

10. Did Shakespeare invent or at least heighten these contrasts for the sake of dramatic effect, or are the pictures
of Italians and Jews true to the racial characteristics
as you know them ? Do you think the poet cared more
or less for verisimilitude of this sort than he did for
dramatic effect ? Establish your answer by citations
from other plays.

11. What opportunities had Shakespeare for the study of
the Italian temperament? Of the Jewish ? Compare
the Venetian temper and spirit as presented in this play
with that presented in *Othello*, I, 3. Account for differences, real or apparent.

12. State what seems to you the central theme or general
idea of the entire play. In how many of the separate
actions is this theme elaborated? In how many is it
merely touched upon ?

13. Try to state concisely the artistic effect or "atmosphere" of the play. What is the mood in which it
leaves you ? By what essential quality do you remember it when you have not read it for some time?

14. Can you see any illustration in this play of Horace
Walpole's famous *mot*, " Life is a comedy to him who
thinks ; a tragedy to him who feels " ?

DETAILED QUESTIONS

I, 1.

1. What do you learn of the character and situation of
Antonio in 1–56 ? What is the chief purpose of these
lines ?

2. Paraphrase 95–102.

3. Are 79–102 intended as characterization of Antonio,

of Gratiano, or of both? Do you think Bassanio speaks
the truth of Gratiano? Compare Gratiano's loquacity
with that of Salarino. What effect has the loquacity of
Antonio's friends, together with Bassanio's comment,
upon your estimate of Antonio?

4. What connection is there between the meaning of "innocence" in l. 145 and the common meaning of the word?
Study and compare the etymology and history of the
words "simple" and "silly." Paraphrase or explain
144b–145.

5. What is your estimate of Bassanio at the end of the
scene?

6. Of Antonio?

7. What is the emotional effect of Antonio's engaging to
trust Bassanio with further sums? To what is this effect
due? What is its dramatic value or purpose?

8. Exposition in this scene?

I, 2.

1. What, exactly, is the tone of the conversation between
Portia and Nerissa? What is the effect of Portia's
criticism of the four suitors?

2. What is gained in probability in having the four suitors
depart without a choice? Is their departure probable
in itself? Why is this a matter of little importance?

3. Exposition in this scene? Is it introduced as deftly as
in the preceding scene?

I, 3.

1. What is Bassanio's manner with Shylock? How much
of this does Shylock feel and what is his response to it?

2. Why does not Bassanio understand at once Shylock's
use of the word "good"? Do you see any subtle characterization here?

3. Explain, by reference to the customs of his race, Shylock's distrust of sea commerce. What preparation is
there in this?

4. Define the two senses of "be assured" in lines 29 and
30.

5. Explain the punctuation of l. 43.

*6. Comment upon the history of "interest," as illustrating l. 52. Compare 62–63. See Bacon's essay *Of Usury*.

7. Can you explain Shylock's apparent hesitation, his reference to Tubal, and his constant naming of the sum asked for? What is the effect of this upon Antonio, in l. 106, and, earlier, upon Bassanio?

8. What is the evidence that Shylock tells the truth in 107–120? If it be truth, where does your sympathy lie in what follows — with Shylock or with Antonio? Or is it divided? Why and how? Did the poet wish it to be divided?

9. What popular prejudice of the poet's time made a division of sympathy here less dangerous to the success of the play than it would be to-day?

10. Outline from the beginning the very clever plan of action by which Shylock works upon the emotions, prejudices, and irritabilities of Antonio and Bassanio so as to get what he wants.

11. We have been made uneasy and solicitous for Antonio in I, 1. How and by how much is this feeling intensified by this scene?

12. How are Acts I and III linked by 181–182? Note that Antonio does not appear again, except for a moment, until after his arrest.

II, 1.

1. Estimate the character of the Prince of Morocco. How does he compare with the other suitors mentioned? Compare him with Shakespeare's other Moor, Othello. What preparation do you find in his character as presented here for his choice among the caskets?

2. Why are we given so much talk about suitors to Portia in I, 2, and why is one here presented in person? Would the poet's purpose have been served as well if the Prince had been made less noble and less intelligent? Explain.

3. If the Moor's hazard is not to be made until "after dinner," why is this scene, without action, inserted here?

4. Explain the lack of parallelism in "blest" and "cursed'st" — one positive and the other superlative — in l. 46.

II, 2.

1. Where and what have we heard of Launcelot before? Is this primarily a verbal humor, or does it depend chiefly upon whimsical character and upon action?
2. For what purposes is this scene introduced? How does it link the story of the caskets with that of Jessica? How does it increase anxiety for Antonio? Why is Gratiano introduced at the end of the scene?

II, 3.

1. What purposes are served in this scene?

II, 4.

1. Explain the talk about preparation for a masque and the appearance of the friends in masks in II, 6. Compare with this, II, 6, 64.

II, 5.

1. With 29–30 compare V, 1, 83–88.
2. Is Shylock more or less appealing and does he attract more or less sympathy in this scene than in I, 3? Why? Do you find any inconsistency in the two presentations?
3. Define the two different phases of Shylock's mind and character. By what means are these differing effects secured? For what purpose?
4. Enumerate the contrasts and antagonisms between Shylock and his Venetian environment as shown in this scene.

II, 6.

1. What bearing have 5–7 upon events in the play other than those which the speaker has in mind, and more important? Is this true of the entire passage, 1–19?
2. Does Gratiano add anything of importance in 8–19 to

the statement made by Salarino in 5–7? Characterize
this speech and compare it with the speeches of Salanio,
Salarino, and Gratiano in I, 1. Can you bring to bear
any evidence that Shakespeare's own mind works in
this fashion and that, instead of being content with one
statement of an idea, he frequently elaborates it almost
beyond recognition, allowing his fancy to run on from
image to image until the idea to be expressed is lost in
the wilderness of expression? *Richard II*, II, 1, 5–16,
is a good example. If you decide that this is a general characteristic of the poet's style, try to determine
whether it is more evident in the early or in the late
plays.

3. Is this a fault of style? To what habit of mind is it
   due? Is it a characteristic of romantic or of classic art,
   primarily? Of youth or of maturity?

4. Propose an explanation of the metrical peculiarity of
   l. 24.

5. Paraphrase and explain 41–42.

6. Is there any moral excuse for Jessica's theft from her
   father? Any dramatic excuse? Are the moral and the
   dramatic aspects of the act two different things? Should
   they be? Would they be so considered and so treated
   by Shakespeare in a tragedy?

7. Explain again, as above, the dramatic value of the
   preparations for the masque which is suddenly called off.

8. Enumerate the several lines of action that have been
   started thus far in the play.

II, 7.

1. Do you think it is a fault of this scene that it has so
   little action and so little fire, enthusiasm and beauty
   even of diction? Why?

2. How has the poet managed the matter of sympathy for
   the Moor, and why? If the Moor was not to engage
   sympathy and not to be treated with all the poet's power,
   why was he given any place in the play? The same
   question applies to the suitors who are not even presented, but of whom we hear in I, 2.

3. What is accomplished by this scene? Why is it placed
   here rather than after II, 1? Compare 44b–45a of the
   latter scene. How does this scene increase suspense?

II, 8.

1. Dramatic value of 25–26a? How is Antonio implicated
   in the elopement of Jessica?
2. Compare 36–45 with II, 6, 5–7, and comment.
3. Chief purpose of this scene?

II, 9.

1. How is suspense sustained by and throughout this
   scene? What is the advantage of presenting a second
   suitor and a second choice?
2. What fault in the character of the Prince determines
   his choice? Compare him, in this respect, with the Moor
   as shown in II, 7.
3. What portion of his audience did the poet expect to
   have take seriously the moralizing passages in the casket scenes?
4. Criticize the attitude of Portia during the casket scenes.
5. Enumerate the elements of suspense that have been
   presented up to the end of the second act.

III, 1.

1. Comment upon the syntax of 5–6.
2. Explain the jest in 28–30.
3. Compare 43–52 with 102–112 and comment.
4. Compare 54–76 with I, 3, 107 *ff.* Note similarities in
   thought and expression. Has Shylock a style peculiarly
   his own? Has any other character in the play?
5. What is the danger to the sympathies of the audience
   in these two eloquent speeches? How does the poet cor
   rect this tendency and avoid this danger in the present
   scene?
6. Does Shylock command respect and sympathy when he
   stands as representative of his race or when he stands
   solely for himself and his individual rights? Prove your
   point by citations. Follow out this line of thought. Does

the poet hold a brief against the Jews as a race or against this individual Jew in particular?

III, 2.

1. Paraphrase 1–24.
2. How does Portia's manner in these lines differ from that shown in her previous speeches?
3. Why are not the inscriptions on the caskets read as in previous scenes? By what device is the omission concealed?
4. Trace the association of ideas in 73–107.
5. Does Bassanio reveal his nature in his choice as clearly as do the Moor and the Prince?
6. How much do we know of the character of Bassanio? Is he revealed in the more favorable light by what he says and does or by his friend's attitude toward him?
7. What can be said for and against the probability or dramatic propriety of 116–130? Does the poet show a profound knowledge of the painter's art here?
8. In what ways would 150–177 be more pleasing to an Elizabethan than to a modern audience? Why?
9. What is the artistic effect of the parallel courtship between Gratiano and Nerissa?

III, 3.

1. What is the purpose and effect of this scene?

III, 4.

1. Mention other plays in which Shakespeare used the device referred to in 60–78. Discuss its effectiveness and utility, remembering that the parts of women were taken by boys in Shakespeare's theater.

III, 5.

1. For what mechanical purpose was this scene inserted? Does it advance the action? Is it interesting for itself? Compare II, 2. Note that in both cases the outdoor scene stands between two indoor scenes.

IV, 1.

1. What preparation has been made for the Duke's attitude?

2. With 6–13 compare III, 2, 296–299. In how many ways does the character of Antonio remind you of the old Roman ideal of manhood?

3. What great modern, almost contemporary, English poem is recalled by l. 66?

4. Comment upon the propriety of the pun in l. 123, considering the attendant circumstances. How could it have been made intelligible in speech?

5. How could Portia know that the Duke had sent for Bellario? Is this an important matter? Is it a matter more easily discernible to a reader than to a spectator? For which was the poet writing?

6. Scan l. 173. Illustrate the connection between " through " and " thorough."

7. What leads to the use of the word "strained" in l. 184? Its meaning here?

8. To what do you attribute the magical imitative effect of 185–186a?

9. Read aloud 184–205 many times, until you have satisfied yourself with the inflection, time, and pitch given to each syllable. This is the sort of exercise that looks easy and is exceedingly difficult. It is also of the utmost value and importance. Memorize the passage.

10. Is the great force and appeal of this passage due primarily to the fact that it enunciates a noble ethical doctrine or to the fact that it clothes great moral truth in a beautifully fitting garment of poetry? Might not every essential idea of the passage be put into a sermon that would be hopelessly dull and uninspiring?

11. To what plea or argument or mental attitude of Shylock's is this speech an answer? How does it illustrate the contrast between the Hebraism of the Old Testament and the Christianity of the New Testament? Compare 228–230a.

an eye for an eye & a tooth for a tooth
Saul —

12. Explain the plural sense of "balance" in l. 255.

13. Compare 315–316 with 184–205 and comment.

*14. In what essential respects does the court procedure differ from that of to-day? What was the method of remunerating lawyers in ancient Greece and Rome? In Shakespeare's day? What connection has this matter with the fall of Sir Francis Bacon?

15. Show that in 449–451, as elsewhere, Antonio's nobility is evinced rather by what he refrains from saying than in what he says. Contrast him, in this respect, with his associates. Why is it peculiarly difficult to show, in drama, the nobility of reticence? Is this one reason why the character of Antonio is, at first acquaintance, somewhat disappointing, or even uninteresting?

IV, 2.

1. At the end of this act, what suspense remains unsatisfied, what action unclosed? Of how long standing is this action? Is it of sufficient interest and importance to sustain the entire concluding act? Or were its lightness and triviality expressly designed to conclude the play in the tone of comedy, which has been endangered by Act IV?

V, 1.

1. To what elements do the first four speeches owe their poetic beauty? Comment especially upon the third — 9–12.

2. What is the effect of the classical allusions — especially as following close upon the tense and painful courtroom scene?

3. Trace closely the association of ideas leading the speakers down from ancient Troy to their own affairs.

4. What bearing have these opening lines upon the question as to whether Shakespeare had ever traveled in Italy?

5. Do the entrances of the messenger and the clown disturb or increase the effect of quiet and magical beauty?

6. How does the poet wrest to poetic uses the very poverty of his stage setting in 54–62, 89–90, 92 and 100? Commit to memory 58–65.

7. What is the common situation of all those present which makes them unusually susceptible to the beauty of the night? Note 107–108.

8. Compare 124–126 with l. 92.

9. Is unity of tone preserved throughout the remainder of this act?

MUCH ADO ABOUT NOTHING

GENERAL QUESTIONS

1. Enumerate the actions of the plot. Trace their inter-relations. Which is the main action? How does the treatment of one of the subplots protract the suspense of the main action? How does the climax of the main action force the solution of one of the subplots?

2. How many days elapse during the action? How many days are actually shown? Point out instances of econ-omy in time. Where might a less careful artist have felt that he needed more time than is used here? Do you find instances of artificial hastening of events?

3. How does the action grow out of past events? What suggestions do you find, especially in Act I, that the chief persons of the drama have been long acquainted? Why is this done? In general, discuss the divergence between the actual time, which the poet records carefully, and the apparent time, the illusion of which he builds up with equal care and with astonishing dex-terity. Do you know of any other Shakespearean play in which this divergence is found?

4. Cite instances of economy in character and incident. Note, for example, that Don John's intrigue is utilized twice — once to provide dramatic entanglement and again to bring Benedick and Beatrice together. This is an admirable example of economy in incident. How does the Benedick-Beatrice plot play into, support, and contrast with the main plot, so as to give a beautiful effect of dramatic unity? How is the " low comedy " welded into the main action?

5. Point out both tragic and farcical material in the action of the play. Do these interact and are they colored and manipulated in such a way as to produce the

effect of pure comedy? Point out several places in which the poet is in danger of producing a tragical or a farcical effect. How does he escape this danger, in each instance? What two characters are conceived not at all in the spirit of tragedy, nor in that of farce, but of pure comedy? Does this explain the prominence given to them?

6. By what means has the villainy of Don John and Borachio been robbed of tragic effect? How would the poet's treatment of this villainy have differed had he been writing a tragedy?

7. Define carefully the spirit or atmosphere created by the first two acts and enumerate in some detail the various touches to which it is due.

8. Study the character contrasts in the play. What use is made of them? For example, how does the character of Benedick assist in the portrayal of the very difficult character of Claudio and help us to make a more just and sympathetic estimate of Claudio's action? Do you think this device of character contrast is overdone in the case of Beatrice and Hero? That is, does it defeat the poet's purpose and endanger the preëminence of the heroine? Is this true also in the case of Benedick and Claudio? How was a similar danger avoided in *Romeo and Juliet?*

9. By what means does the poet try to soften the unduly tragic effect of his main-plot material? In this connection, consider: low-comedy relief; the shallowness of Claudio and Hero; the nature of their love; the verbal frivolity and persiflage of Benedick and Beatrice; the postponement of the rejection scene to the fourth act and the hurried conclusion which leaves no time for reflection; the general evasion of moral issues. It is clear that the poet uses great ingenuity. Does he succeed?

10. What sort of apology is made for the ugly action of Claudio? Note the insistence upon his extreme youth in I, 1, 12–15, and follow up this suggestion throughout the play. In what sense is Claudio hero of the play?

What similar problem did the poet face in connection with Hero and how did he solve it?

11. How and why does this play fail to satisfy the demands of the Spirit of Comedy as *Twelfth Night* and *As You Like It* satisfy it?

*12. Read George Meredith's essay *On the Uses of the Comic Spirit* and criticize this play in the light of the ideal there expressed.

DETAILED QUESTIONS

I, 1.

1. Point out cases of affected alliteration, antithesis, and " euphuism " in the messenger's speeches. Where does Leonato return in kind? How does this prepare for the verbal fencing of Benedick and Beatrice?

2. Note all references to past time. Purpose and effect of these? Note also that Claudio's uncle, named in 18–25, does not appear in the play. Why is he mentioned? What is the effect of the nick-name by which Beatrice refers to Benedick? Compare 119–120.

3. What exposition in 1–95? Why does this precede the entrance of Don Pedro and his company?

4. Explain Benedick's motive in 125–128. What is the motive behind the reply? Are the two speakers sincere? Compare 167–170.

5. With 158–159 compare *King Lear*, II, 2, 101b–110. If this were a tragedy, what result should we expect from this dalliance of the forces of good with the forces of evil? What result do we anticipate here, in a comedy, and what is the dramatic effect produced? (Much would depend, of course, upon the stage appearance and make-up of the villain.)

*6. How does Benedick tempt the Nemesis of comedy in 240 *ff.*? What do his boastful protestations lead us to expect? Note that he is affecting a peculiarity of exemption from the most powerful and inevitable law of nature. The arrows of comedy are levelled most unerringly against singularities of this sort and against all that offends common sense. Compare the central idea of *Love's Labour's Lost*.

7. Explain the change to verse after l. 291. Comment upon the differences in prose rhythm between the speeches of Benedick and Claudio in 172–205.

*8. Compare the relations existing between Claudio and Don Pedro with those between Bassanio and Antonio in the *Merchant of Venice*. With Benedick in this scene compare Mercutio in *Romeo and Juliet*.

9. Infer from l. 296 the depth of Claudio's passion. What bearing has this upon later events? Is such a love likely to afford material for tragedy?

10. What exposition in this scene? What action is started? Note the dexterity with which exposition and action are interwoven.

I, 2.

1. With this mention of Antonio's son, who does not appear, compare I, 1, 18–25, and comment.

2. What advantage is gained by the distortion of fact in 7–16?

3. Purpose and effect of this scene? Compare *Romeo and Juliet*, I, 5.

I, 3.

1. What is the underlying cause of Don John's mood as presented in 1–42? Why is the poet so careful to reveal this mood and its cause? What further motive do you discover in 42–77?

2. Comment upon the profound insight shown by the poet in 73–74.

*3. Is Don John a dangerous villain, like Iago? What are his relations with his followers? Does he reveal his real nature to them? Compare Iago.

4. How many conferences have there been between Don Pedro and Claudio? After reading I, 2, 7–16, and I, 3, 60–66, criticize the stage setting of I, 1, found in most editions, but due to modern editors, " Before Leonato's House."

5. What complicating factor is added to the action in this scene?

II, 1.

1. How many times has Beatrice seen Don John, so far as the play indicates? But what is the implication of 4–6? Purpose of this?

2. What material of I, 1, are Beatrice's speeches in 1–86 intended to parallel? How is the character of Hero shown in these lines?

3. Read over all of Antonio's previous speeches and comment upon 126–127.

4. With 155–156 compare I, 1, 50–52.

5. How do 90–160 advance the action or give new insight into character? Have these lines any other purpose?

6. Since 167–189 lead to nothing, why are they used? What insight do they give into the character of Claudio? How do they imitate, in little, the action of the play and induce a receptive attitude toward what is difficult to believe in that action? This is one of Shakespeare's cleverest dramatic devices.

7. Comment upon the irony of 185–186a. Why are 179–189 in verse?

8. With 182–184 compare sonnets 40–42 and *Two Gentlemen of Verona*, V, 4, 53b–54a.

9. Why is Benedick so much more voluble against Beatrice in 246–280 than he was when in her presence?

10. What great romantic enthusiasm of Shakespeare's time is reflected and mildly ridiculed in 271–280?

11. How is the illusion of dramatic time heightened in 287–291?

12. Is it clear from this scene that Hero has expected to be the bride of Don Pedro and that she accepts Claudio as a substitute? Why is she made so morally worthless?

13. What considerations of probability necessitated the postponement of the wedding? Note the care with which the action is dated.

II, 2.

1. What bearing have 12–14 upon the illusion of dramatic time?

2. How are the two plots or intrigues now under way connected, if at all? How are they contrasted in the motives behind them?

II, 3.

1. What instances of irony in 5–58? How much of this would be appreciated by an audience ignorant of the outcome?

2. Explain the change to verse in l. 39.

*3. Does it seem significant that Benedick is no lover of music? Compare the same trait in Hotspur, Othello, and Prince Hal. But see *Merchant of Venice*, V, 1, 70 *ff*. To what class of men did Shakespeare ascribe this dislike of music or indifference to it? Where did the poet's own sympathies lie? Note that even in his mockery Benedick is made to give powerful expression to the mystery of musical influence, just as Theseus really praises poetry in his attempt to condemn it.

4. What is the relation of the song to the main theme of the play? What person of the drama, not present on the stage, is represented in mood and manner by the song?

5. What twofold appeal is made to the eavesdropping Benedick in 91–217? How is this shown in 228–255? With 239–245 compare 26–38.

6. What parallelism and contrast do you find between 5–58 and 228–255?

7. Can you date this scene?

III, 1.

1. How and why is Margaret kept out of this plot?

2. Would the simile in 7–11a assist the audience in imagining the "pleached bower," which was represented on the stage, if at all, in only the vaguest symbolic fashion? Criticize the simile on the ground of good

taste. What do you think may have led the poet to write it?

3. Point out, in 1–36, several passages tending to give the scene a tone and feeling of the open air. What similar effects do you recall from other plays?

4. Comment upon the irony in 84–87.

5. Explain the blank verse in this scene as against the prose in the preceding. Why is the scene shorter than II, 3?

6. Do Hero and Ursula make the same appeals to Beatrice as were made before to Benedick? Explain differences. How does Beatrice's response differ from Benedick's?

7. What is the date of this scene? See 100–101.

III, 2.

1. With 1–75 compare II, 3, 243 ff. With 43–49 compare II, 1, 31–40.

2. Study very carefully Claudio's manner when he hears the calumny against Hero. Why did the poet think it necessary to make him so dastardly? To what elements of his character does Don John successfully appeal?

3. Study the attitudes of the two half brothers towards each other. What peculiarity of Don John's becomes of value to the poet at this point?

4. Point out two lines of contrast between the two parts of this scene.

5. On what day does the action of this scene occur?

III, 3.

*1. Why is the character of Verges added to that of Dogberry? Compare Justices Shallow and Silence in *II Henry IV*, Shallow and Slender in *The Merry Wives*, Rosencrantz and Guildenstern in *Hamlet*. In the present couple, what nice shadings of difference are discernible?

2. What special delight, nearly lost to us, would an Elizabethan audience take in 1–101? Discuss the propriety

of making these watchmen so patently English in character and manner. Mention similar features in other plays. This is Shakespeare's almost constant practice in low comedy scenes. What did he gain by it and what did he lose? Do you think he felt that while pathos and wit are cosmopolitan and universal, humor is more likely to be local or racial? Is there a possible connection between this practice and the fact that low comedy was of native English growth while high comedy was an importation, as to form, matter, and spirit, from Europe?

3. What evidence in Borachio's speeches that he is drunk? Note that his name is close to the Spanish for "wineskin" or "drunkard" and was used in the latter sense in England for a century after Shakespeare's time.

*4. What varying effects of intoxication are shown: in Cassio, *Othello*, II, 3; in Lepidus, *Antony and Cleopatra*, II, 7; in Shallow and in Silence, *II Henry IV*, V, 3; in Caliban, *Tempest*, III, 2; in Falstaff, *I* and *II Henry IV* and *Merry Wives, passim*? Is the last a good example? Why?

5. What advantages, in the way of probability, are gained by presenting Borachio drunk?

6. How is the tragic effect of Don John's plot and of IV, 1, softened by the detection made in this scene? But how is suspense retained, at the same time, by the manner and instruments of that detection? This is but one touch out of the many that make the present play one of the most consummate pieces of stage-craft.

III, 4.

1. What is the purpose of this scene? With what earlier scene is it parallel? What is indicated by the mood of Hero?

III, 5.

1. How does this scene weld the low comedy into the main plot? How does it increase suspense? What is the significance of its position just before IV, 1?

2. Study the psychology and character of Dogberry.

3. Why is it necessary that Leonato should not know of Don John's intrigue until after IV, 1 ? Show, then, that the characters of Dogberry and Verges were designed to meet precisely this exigency of the plot.

IV, 1.

1. Explain the change to verse in l. 23. What elements of theatrical posing and false rhetoric do you find in Claudio's speeches ?

*2. Study very carefully Hero's reaction in this renunciation scene. Is it that of a person of any moral worth or strength ? Note that earlier in the play she has accepted Claudio in lieu of Don Pedro, under paternal orders, with perfect sweetness and equanimity. Does the poet wish us to sympathize with her deeply ? Compare Desdemona and Imogen.

3. What can be said in favor of Claudio and Hero in this scene ? Notice their youth, docility, self-respect, conscious purity. Do you find their virtues vivid and positive or futile and sterile ?

4. What dramatic value do you find in the easy credulity of Leonato ? Is this attitude of his in keeping with his character as it has been shown before ?

5. Explain the use of "shall" and "will" in l. 211.

6. Does the Friar advance any reason for his plan other than that mentioned in 212–213 ? What incident in 'Romeo and Juliet does this plan recall ? Compare the two.

7. Comment upon the action of Benedick and Beatrice in 1–256.

8. Explain the change to prose in l. 257. What is the mood of Benedick and what is that of Beatrice at the opening of their interview ? How is this mood colored by : their former relations; the intrigue of the Prince to bring them together ; the climax of the main plot just preceding ?

9. What has been the chief obstacle to their love hitherto ? How is this removed by the experience of Hero ?

10. How do 257–340 join the serious and the comic plots insolubly together and wrest Don John's tragic intrigue

to comic uses? Note, however, that in this contact, a touch of tragedy is communicated from the one to the other. What is this? Meantime, what tincture of comedy is spreading over the Don John intrigue?

11. How do 257–340 serve as a modulation from the key of 1–256 to that of IV, 2? What stage is marked in the comic plot by these lines?

12. Carefully review this scene, one of the most masterly and famous in Shakespeare's theater, making an estimate of its richness and variety in mood, motive, emotion, character, and poetry.

13. Why should this scene be called the climax of the play? (The chief reason for the postponement of the climax until the fourth act seems to lie in the tragic coloring of the main plot and the consequent necessity of hastening to a conclusion appropriate to comedy before the moral question becomes too pressing.)

IV, 2.

1. What person present at this trial scene assures us at once, so that we may enjoy the fun, that there will be no repetition of former blunders?

2. By what means has Dogberry been raised to the duties of magistrate? Does he appear familiar with those duties? What has been the effect upon him of his new dignities? What is the cause of his indignant outburst in 76 *ff.*? Is there an unintentional pun in l. 77?

3. Why was this scene made to follow immediately upon IV, 1?

V, 1.

1. With 35–36 compare III, 2, 28–30. With l. 26, compare III, 2, 72. Do you think such correspondencies are accidental or do they serve some æsthetic purpose? Compare the reminiscential themes in orchestral music, frequently employed to bind together the movements of a symphony.

2. Comment upon the speeches of Antonio, 80–109, as a study in old age. What effect have they upon Leonato?

3. Does Claudio's manner toward Benedick in 111 *ff.* show that he has no qualms of conscience regarding his treatment of Hero?

4. Paraphrase 207–208a. What is Don Pedro's thought in 208b–209? How does this speech serve as transition and preparation?

5. With l. 300, compare I, 2, 1–2, and explain.

6. Comment upon 302b–304a. But when has Hero been guilty of precisely the same contemptible levity? Take the hero's final measure from "poor Claudio" in l. 305.

7. How does the bait held out here resemble that which lured Claudio in I, 1, 296–297? Does Shakespeare even make Leonato guilty of a lie in regard to Antonio's children in order to make it clear that Claudio values not the girl but her wealth? Compare I, 2, 1–2.

8. Give more than one explanation of the change in Borachio since his last appearance. Does it seem likely that Margaret would have been ignorant of the grounds of the accusation against Hero and therefore unable to clear her character? How is this difficulty managed? Note that Margaret does not appear in Act IV and that in V, 2, she seems ignorant of details.

9. Before taking leave of the immortal Dogberry and his crew, make an estimate of their place in the mechanics of the play and of what they have done to hold the tragic plot down to the comic level.

V, 2.

1. Does Margaret's levity seem in keeping with her mistress's recent experience? Is it intended to indicate that she did not know of that experience and thereby to explain why she failed to exculpate Hero? Compare V, 4, 4–7. Or is Shakespeare careless of these minor details, knowing that they are of little consequence in rapid stage action, never dreaming that his text would ever be examined minutely? Is he not chiefly concerned in bringing his play to a swift conclusion in a tone of light-hearted banter?

2. Comment upon Benedick's singing. Compare II, 3, 60–63, and also III, 2, 60–62.

3. What is accomplished in this scene?

V, 3.

1. On what day and at what hour does this scene take place? Compare V, 1, 295, and see 24–27. What is the symbolic significance of this? Note that it is a device not often employed by Shakespeare. It is more in the manner of Maeterlinck.

2. Compare this scene, for theatrical effect, with IV, 1. Both scenes are dominated by the sentimental egoist, Claudio. How do 32–33 intensify this effect, showing that he has enjoyed the spectacle of his own "woe"?

V, 4.

1. What is the cause of Benedick's "February face"? Compare 25–27.

2. Is Benedick like most jesters in disliking a jest turned against himself? Compare II, 1, 246–269; II, 3, 245–252, and 101–113 of the present scene. What evidence is there that Beatrice is like him in this? How does this common trait afford suspense even in the last scene?

3. It has been said that "we should make haste to laugh lest we begin to weep." It is probably true that there is no comedy which, by logical prolongation, would fail to end in tragedy. How does Shakespeare's somewhat mechanical truncation of the action of this play illustrate this point and at the same time satisfy our sense of poetic justice? There are clouds of tragedy lurking below the horizon, but we are content to "think not on them till to-morrow."

4. Did Shakespeare think, in your opinion, that this play should end as it does, or did he force his material, perhaps somewhat unwillingly, into a preëxisting mould — the mould of comedy? Does your answer apply to all the play or to the last act chiefly? Can you recall other plays of his in which you feel the same thing? Are they comedies or tragedies?

AS YOU LIKE IT

GENERAL QUESTIONS

1. Enumerate the actions or stories of the plot and the various groups into which the persons of the drama fall. Which of these are principal and which subordinate? With what incident does the main action originate? With what incidents does it culminate?

2. What stories or episodes might have been eliminated without loss to the play?

3. Cite as many evidences as possible of haste or careless-ness on the poet's part — evidences that he is playing with his characters. Note especially Act V. Is the char-acter of Touchstone consistent with itself throughout?

4. What characters seem to be of little dramatic value — mere " walking gentlemen who serve to fill up a world"? What characters are treated with greatest care and in-sight? What characters are treated with manifest sym-pathy and delight? What characters, necessary to the machinery of the play, are blocked in hastily?

5. Write a carefully considered estimate of Jaques. Why does he do nothing? Is he sincere? Does he at all re-semble Touchstone? What do you know or infer as to his past? How and why did he fall into his present company? Compare V, 4, 190–191. Compare him with Hamlet. Does any one like him? Is any one indifferent towards him? Compare him with any of the other char-acters for reality and " convincing " quality. Can you explain Shakespeare's obvious interest in him?

6. What parts of the action are improbable? What parts are clearly impossible? To what degree do these con-siderations mar the effect of the play? Have they the same effect as the improbabilities and impossibilities that compose the whole tissue of *A Midsummer Night's Dream*?

7. How many instances do you find in this play of love at first sight? How does the use of this device economize time and incident? Since love at first sight is itself an improbability, would you consider these several instances of it, occurring at one time and place, as one of the play's most staggering impossibilities?

8. The defects of the play have been only vaguely suggested in the foregoing questions. It is not well planned, it is weak in action, thin in portraiture, unequal in interest, and shows little of the poet's stern power of precise and logical thought. Yet it remains one of the most perennially fresh and pleasing plays in the world. Why?

DETAILED QUESTIONS

I, 1.

1. What exposition in this scene? Is it easily and naturally introduced? Especially in 1–27? Does Oliver hear for the first time the "old news" mentioned in 103–109? Then why recount it here?

2. What is the value of the reference to "Robin Hood of England"? Compare *Hamlet*, V, 1, 161–162.

3. What are we to understand from the fact that Oliver expects Charles, as shown in 94–95 and 128–131? Does this show that the plot has been laid already? How does this device accelerate the action? Compare Act I of *King Lear*, where it is clear that the distribution of lands has already been made.

4. Explain the tempered treatment of the villainy of Oliver and Charles. How and why would it have been differently treated if this were a tragedy? Compare *Macbeth*, III, 1, 75 *ff.*, *Hamlet*, IV, 7, 58 *ff.*, and *The Tempest*, II, 1, 205 *ff.*

5. Do you find 169–180 natural and convincing? What is the dramatic purpose of the passage? Compare the first speech of Richard III in the play of that name.

I, 2.

1. Why is the report of Charles's earlier bouts given here?
   Show that the awkward device of shifting the wrestling ground was forced upon the poet if he wished to present the results of the earlier bouts.
2. How is Rosalind distinguished from Celia in this scene? Comment closely upon 284–287. Compare I, 3, 117.
3. Why are both Orlando and Rosalind in just the mood for love at first sight?
4. What exposition in this scene?

I, 3.

1. What is the purpose of 1–40? Do you think Rosalind's manner entirely pleasing here?
2. What preparation has been made for the banishment of Rosalind?
3. Is Duke Frederick's treatment of Rosalind adequately explained? Compare I, 2, 236–242.
4. Show that in 71–86 there is, at one and the same time, characterization of each of the three persons present, and exposition.
5. With 111b–124 compare *Merchant of Venice*, III, 4, 60–78.
6. What incongruity, as to time, between l. 73 and I, 1, 100–125?

II, 1.

1. How does this scene contrast in tone with the scene preceding and the one following? What is its tone? What is its importance for the play?
*2. How were the first three scenes of this act staged at the Globe Theater?

II, 3.

1. Paraphrase and discuss 10–11.
2. How does the poet's treatment of Oliver resemble that

of Duke Frederick? Did he care greatly about this?
Why?

3. What elements go to make the great charm of this
scene?

II, 4.

1. Why are Corin and Silvius introduced here? What is
the function of the clown?

2. Discuss this scene as a varied and many-sided treatment of the theme of love.

3. How is the tone and temper of II, 1, recalled here?
By the end of this scene we have definitely entered the
land of illusion. The spirit of the forest dominates the
rest of the play. Outline the steps by which the transition has been made from the outer world of reality to
this world of dream.

II, 5.

1. What action or "business" accompanies 60–61?

2. How does this scene advance characterization? Has it
any other purpose? What is its relation to scene 7?
Note 32b–33 and 64.

II, 6.

1. How were scenes 5, 6, and 7 staged in Shakespeare's
theater? Note that the banquet is prepared at the end
of scene 5 and that it must appear again in scene 7, but
not in scene 6.

II, 7.

1. What two actions are connected by Jaques's meeting
with the fool? Explain, as far as possible, his expressions of delight in the fool. Are they wholly sincere?
Does he realize his resemblance to the fool?

2. Read over 12–34 many times, until you have mastered
every turn of thought and inflection of voice. Note
especially the beautifully ductile rhythm. What mood
in the speaker does this rhythm seem to you to indicate?

3. What governs Orlando's choice of items in 114–117?

Why does the duke repeat this part of Orlando's speech almost *verbatim*?

4. Explain the popularity of 139b–166. What can be said against it? What do you infer as to the character and previous experience of the speaker? Did Shakespeare admire the speaker?

5. Is this famous speech dramatic? Is it an integral part of the play and of the present situation, or is it an excrescence?

6. Would a speech of this length, having no relation to the action and merely amplifying a chance remark by another speaker, be tolerated on the modern stage? As a matter of fact, it goes very lamely to-day because it is addressed to the group on the stage. In Shakespeare's theater it was recited to the audience. Point out other similar speeches in the scene. Who speaks them?

7. What is the fitness of the song for the situation?

8. What instance of dramatic economy do you find at the end of the scene?

III, 1.

1. What is the irony in Duke Frederick's treatment of Oliver? What is the irony in Oliver's situation?

2. How does this scene advance the action?

III, 2.

1. How do 1–19 differ in form from a Shakespearean sonnet? Why was the speech written in rhymed verse?

2. Where does Orlando suppose Rosalind to be?

3. Show that there is, after all, much sound sense in 13–23. Compare carefully II, 1, 1–18. What is intended in this contrast?

4. What purpose is served in the comparison of court and country? In what way does Touchstone rather remotely resemble Jaques in this passage?

5. With "palm-tree" in l. 186, compare 377–380. With II, 1, 21–25, compare IV, 3, 115. Comment upon the flora and fauna of the wood. How does it harmonize with the spirit of the play? Of course this feature was

derived from Shakespeare's source, but do you think it
was retained through carelessness or by design?

6. The actual scene of the play is foreign. Present all the
evidence tending to show that Shakespeare wished his
audience to think of England chiefly, in these forest
scenes. What popular English hero, familiar in ballad
and story, would be called to mind during these scenes?
Where is the Forest of Arden? Where is the Forest of
Ardennes? Had Shakespeare any reasons, connected
with his parentage, for being particularly interested in
the former?

7. Did the poet intend that either of the antagonists should
be clearly victorious in the contest of 268–311? Why?
Comment upon 293–299.

8. Guess Rosalind's purpose in l. 267 in the light of what
she does in 312–315. Why did she wish to get Celia
out of the way? Note her comparative boldness. Compare I, 2, 257–260, and 264–267.

9. Comment upon Rosalind's attempt at wit in 331–351.
Why was it probably intended to fall rather flat? Why
are 331–335 slightly off the part that she is playing?

10. Comment upon the delightful humor of 369–377a.

11. Shakespeare is very fond of the sort of dramatic irony
illustrated in 406–410. In V, 4, it runs riot. Do you
think it very effective? Give reasons why it would be
more successful on the stage than in reading. What is
the source of one's pleasure in such stock devices?

12. How does Rosalind strengthen her *incognito* in 427–445?

13. What is the central improbability in this whole scene
between the lovers?

14. Why does not Rosalind reveal herself at once to Orlando? Because she delights in the game she is playing, or because in Shakespeare's time audiences de-
manded full five acts for their money?

III, 3.

1. Does it seem fitting that Touchstone should liken himself to Ovid, and especially that he should make the
learned pun upon "capricious"?

2. Is it possible that in 12–17 Shakespeare is wresting the words out of Touchstone's mouth and is really writing, with a bitter smile, about certain Stratford memories of his own?

3. At what other point in this scene does Touchstone seem inconsistent with his character as presented earlier in the play? Note, for example, his moral frivolity in 25–41 and his "euphuism," which, indeed, he might have learned at court, in 61–66.

III, 4.

1. What contrast is there between the disguise and the emotions of Rosalind? What effect was this contrast intended to make? What does Celia try to do here?

2. Comment upon 37–42.

3. What does the speaker intend in l. 62? How is this in character and in harmony with the speaker's present situation?

III, 5.

1. What dramatic irony in this scene?

2. Do you think it natural that Phebe, who has been as adamant to Corin's praises, should soften beneath the scorn and reviling of Rosalind? How does Rosalind nearly betray her sex in 34–63?

3. With the situation here compare *Twelfth Night*, III, 1, 104 *ff.* Why should such a situation be especially effective on Shakespeare's stage?

4. Discuss the propriety and fitness to time, place, and speaker of the reference to Marlowe, 81–82.

5. With l. 130, compare sonnets 127, 130, 131 and *Love's Labour's Lost*, IV, 3, 252–253.

IV, 1.

1. Note that neither Rosalind nor Orlando cares for Jaques's company but that he seems to desire theirs. Yet he poses as a solitary.

*2. What evidence do you find in 1–38 that Jaques' "melancholy" which he attributes to the "sundry contemplation of his travels," was a fashionable affectation of the time of Elizabeth? See Roger Ascham's *The Schole-master*.

3. Why is it appropriate that Orlando should speak in blank verse, in l. 30? Show that Jaques' comment upon this has the effect of strengthening the stage illusion.

4. Explain Celia's motive in 66–67. Is she afraid that Rosalind has been too daring? Or should we here recall I, 3, 114–115a?

*5. In what spirit is classical antiquity treated in 94–108? Compare the spirit of *Troilus and Cressida*, probably written within a year of this play, on the same material.

6. Compare this speech with III, 5, 8–27.

IV, 3.

1. Comment fully upon the conversion of Oliver. Is the cause of this conversion adequate?

2. With 164-165 compare V, 2, 21 and 31. Comment.

3. What is the source of the beautiful pathos in 166–169?

V, 1.

1. To whom does Audrey refer in "old gentleman," l. 4? Why?

2. How does Touchstone resemble Jaques in 11–14?

3. What is Touchstone's purpose in 33–56? Do you see any sense or connection of ideas in 33–40?

V, 2.

1. Does Rosalind, in 32 *ff.*, interpret Orlando's meaning in l. 31, correctly? Is this deliberate? In what ways might these lines be acted?

2. With 11b–14 compare III, 1, 16–18. Comment.

3. Does the interpretation that Orlando recognizes Rosalind through her disguise spoil the rest of the play for you? Why? What evidence is in favor of this interpretation? May we even suppose that Rosalind knows he recognizes her and yet take an even greater pleas-

ure in the closing scenes? Does the poet force any of these interpretations? Why?

4. What is the dramatic value of 114–131?

V, 3.

1. What is the function of this scene?
2. In how many different ways is the beautiful song in keeping with the place, the occasion, and the spirit of the play?

V, 4.

1. Does the poet intend to exhibit an example of woman's logic in 11–14? What is wrong here?
2. What is the dramatic value of 1–25? Compare V, 2, 114–131.
3. What effect is intended in 26–29?
4. Comment upon the humor of 61–64 and 71b–72a. Where has this attitude of Touchstone toward Audrey been noted before? Does he marry her in good faith? Note 57–59 and cite earlier passages to the same effect.
5. Is there any dramatic value in 71–109? That is, does it advance the action or portray character? Is it consistent with Touchstone's character and social position? Is it another hit at fashionable affectations? Note especially 94–95.
6. What satire do you find in 71–109? Kindly or cynical? Compare, in this respect, the satire in Jaques' famous monologue, II, 7, 139–166.
7. Note that the present passage deals with court and city life. Compare III, 2, 12–23, and comment.
8. Criticize and discuss the necessity of Duke Frederick's astonishingly swift and complete conversion. Compare that of Oliver. Show that these things are in harmony with the general tone of the comedy and with its title.
9. What reason can you give for the supposition that Adam took the part of Hymen?
10. Comment upon the lines spoken by Jaques.

Epilogue

1. Note the bewildering confusion in the matter of sex. Here we have a boy speaking who has been acting the part of a girl disguised in man's clothing. In the first line he tells us that " It is not the fashion to see the lady the epilogue," and later he says " If I were a woman" !

TWELFTH NIGHT

GENERAL QUESTIONS

1. Enumerate the actions of the play. Into what groups do the characters fall? Which of these are principal and which subordinate? By what events and characters are these actions and groups interconnected? Whom do you consider the leading characters — those that control and shape the action?

2. Enumerate the love stories presented. Have they any common characteristic? What persons among the chief characters are not in love?

3. What improbabilities do you find in the action? Do any of the characters seem overdrawn?

4. What length of time is supposed to elapse during the play? How many days are actually shown? Is there anything surprising in V, I, 102? Explain.

*5. What situations, incidents, and characters recall similar things in the poet's earlier comedies? A full discussion of this interesting and important topic requires a knowledge of all Shakespeare's comedies down to and including *As You Like It*, but especially of his first three. His most obvious limitation, a comparative poverty of invention, may be illustrated admirably by showing how he works over in the present play, his masterpiece in comedy, the materials of his apprenticeship.

6. More attention is paid to music in this play than in any other by Shakespeare. Gather the references to it. Discuss the part played by the songs in producing the total effect of the comedy.

7. Hazlitt said of this play: "It is perhaps too good-natured for comedy." Does the poet treat any of the characters in a purely satiric way? Or is his manner

kindly and sympathetic throughout? What characters seem to lend themselves to satiric treatment? Was Dr. Johnson right in saying that Sir Andrew is "not the proper prey of a satirist"?

8. To what characters do you feel superior? With what characters have you a feeling of fellowship?

9. Write a brief study of Malvolio. What is meant by calling him a Puritan? (Of course it is clear that the Puritan spirit is independent of time and place. It may be found in ancient Egypt as well as in seventeenth-century London and in Illyria as well as in New England.)

10. Why do all the other characters dislike Malvolio and make a butt of him? Why is he legitimate prey for comedy? George Meredith's famous essay "On the Uses of the Comic Spirit" is helpful here. Show that in his treatment of Malvolio Shakespeare has been very moderate and charitable. The man was nearly everything that the poet disliked. Throughout his life as a dramatist Shakespeare and his friends of the theaters were in more or less open conflict with men of this type of mind — men who thought that because they were virtuous there should be no more cakes and ale. The type is deathless.

11. Why is the part of Malvolio considered the leading male rôle in the play by modern actors?

*12. Do you think this play is, on the whole, nearer the height of Shakespeare's accomplishment in comedy than *Much Ado, Merchant of Venice, As You Like It*? State reasons in each case. Show that each of these is superior to the present play in some particulars. (For sheer intellectual power, *Troilus and Cressida* may be considered the greatest of the comedies.) But *Twelfth Night* is rounded, globed, complete. It exhibits all the poet's comic powers in perfect balance and harmony. It is the master's show piece.

DETAILED QUESTIONS

I, 1.

1. Explain or comment upon the following words in 1–15: " appetite," " fall," " sound," " quick," " that" in l. 10, " capacity," "validity," "pitch," "fancy," "high fantastical."
2. Paraphrase 1–15.
3. Estimate the character of the Duke and his present state of mind from these introductory lines alone. Compare 40–41.
4. What exposition is there in this scene?

I, 2.

1. What is the dramatic value of the captain's narrative in 8–17?
2. Explain "those poor number," l. 10. This is a good illustration of the elasticity of the English language in Shakespeare's time.
3. Comment upon l. 29. Does it show an unpleasant boldness?
4. Place together ll. 29, 34, 41b, 45, 55b, and outline the stages of Viola's thought. Is it fairly clear that the whole plan of her future action is here in embryo? Is she " setting her cap " for the Duke?
5. What exposition do you find in this scene?

I, 3.

1. What is the condition of Sir Toby? Point out several passages in 1–46 that show this.
2. What preparation in these lines for the later marriage of Sir Toby and Maria?
3. Does Sir Toby appear to wish to be rid of Sir Andrew? Why has the latter remained hitherto and what detains him at the present time?
4. What are the relations existing between the two knights? Estimate the character of each as shown in this scene alone.

5. Do you see any special dexterity in stage-craft in 149–151?

6. Why is this scene in prose? What does it add in the way of exposition?

I, 4.

1. What time has elapsed since the action of I, 2?

2. With 13–14 compare *Romeo and Juliet*, I, 3, 81 *ff.*, *Love's Labour's Lost*, IV, 2, 113, and *King John*, II, 1, 485. Comment.

3. What are we to infer from l. 16?

4. Why do Viola's speeches change from prose to verse after the entrance of the Duke?

5. Does Orsino give good and adequate reasons for sending Viola on the mission to Olivia? Does it seem the rational and natural thing to do? Does the poet succeed here in slurring over a slight improbability which is serviceable to his plot?

6. How might the abruptness of Viola's "aside" in 41–42 be softened in acting?

7. What does this scene add to our necessary knowledge of the characters and the situation? Is there any new development?

8. Do you find any dramatic irony in the scene?

I, 5.

1. What is Maria's precise feeling and attitude toward the clown? Does this prepare us to feel likewise?

2. What is Malvolio's attitude toward Feste? Should this have the same weight with us as that of Maria? Is there characterization of some one beside Feste in Malvolio's two speeches regarding him?

3. What is the wisdom and justice of 97–104?

4. What occasions Olivia's change of mind in l. 172? What is the inference as to her character?

5. Is Viola really in doubt as to the identity of Olivia in 177 *ff.*? What, then, is her object in asking?

6. What words of Viola's justify Olivia's question in l. 194?

7. Explain in detail 217–220.

8. By what words in the following twelve lines is the idea started in " divinity," l. 233, carried out?

9. Explain l. 254. Is it the sarcasm of jealousy or is it fully explained in Olivia's previous speech?

10. Comment fully upon the spirit in which 256–261 are spoken. Why in verse? With l. 261 compare sonnet 1.

11. Is the curse uttered in l. 305 carried out? Why? Compare those in *Richard III* or in *King Lear*.

12. Reading back through the scene, show in detail what has been Olivia's attitude toward Viola from the first moment she saw her.

13. How many love stories are we following at this point in the play? Characterize each in a word.

14. How is the action advanced in this scene?

II, 1.

1. Paraphrase 11–17.

2. What is the meaning of " estimable wonder " in l. 29?

3. Is Antonio's affection for Sebastian somewhat over-drawn? Would it have seemed less so to an Elizabethan audience than to us? What purpose does it serve later?

4. Compare 11–12a with 43b–44.

II, 2.

1. Why does Olivia send the ring after Viola?

2. Paraphrase 23b–24.

3. Paraphrase and explain 30–31.

4. What dramatic purpose is served by 18–42?

II, 3.

1. Comment upon Sir Andrew's repeated use of the word " fool " and " fooling " in 15 *ff*. Explain the unintentional pun in l. 89.

*2. Compare 158–166, both as to style and matter, with the " character writing " of the seventeenth century, well represented in Earle's *Microcosmographie* and Samuel Butler's *Characters*. Compare *Troilus and Cressida* I, 2, 20–31. Does Shakespeare seem to have been well acquainted with the technic of the "character"? Were any of the character books in existence as early as this play? See Ben Jonson's *Every Man in His Humour* in this connection.

3. What is gained by outlining the plot against Malvolio before it is put into action?

II, 4.

1. Was not Viola engaged in the Duke's service as a singer? Compare I, 2, 55–59. Does the song suit Viola better than it does the clown? Is it evident from the first lines of the scene that the Duke expected Viola to sing the song? Should the Duke have remembered that it was not Viola but Feste who sang it on the previous evening? Is it natural that Feste should frequent the Duke's palace? Do 8–14 seem like patchwork? Note that they are in prose. What inference do you draw from all this? May it be that the actor now playing the part of Feste originally impersonated Viola and that when he grew up some boy who could not sing was given the part of Viola? Compare I, 4, 32b–34.

2. With 33–36a compare 96–106a. Is this due to negligence on the poet's part or is it characterization? Does it illustrate 75–77?

3. Viola's covert confession of her love, tremblingly poised between woman's reticence and man's candor, is the outstanding *purpurea panna* of the play. Memorize 113b–118.

4. Explain l. 124b.

5. What two earlier scenes are recalled by the present one? How does the Duke's manner here closely resemble that shown in an earlier scene?

II, 5.

+*1. What special significance do you find in Malvolio's dislike of bear-baiting? Compare II, 3, 151. If possible, see Stubbs' *Anatomy of Abuse* upon this sport.

2. How do the asides of the eavesdroppers create suspense in 27–195?

3. With 85–90 compare *Love's Labour's Lost*, I, 1, 250–260 and *Much Ado*, IV, 2, 76–90.

4. How much does Fabian add to the play either here or elsewhere ? Note that the number of actors required for this play is relatively small and give a possible explanation of the inclusion of the part.

III, 1.

1. Is there any special significance in Feste's statement that he lives by the church ? Compare IV, 2, 1–10.

2. How does l. 102 explain l. 78 ?

*3. Explain 108–110. Compare Ben Jonson's assault upon the word " servant " in *The Silent Woman*.

4. Point out numerous instances in this scene of high-flown diction used for its own sake, apparently, but yet coupled with ridicule of it. Has the colloquy of Viola and the clown any purpose other than that of introducing this material ? This is Shakespeare's fairly constant attitude toward speech-embroidery : he sees its futility and æsthetic wrongness but he never quite learns to leave it alone. Perhaps, after all, we should be glad of that.

5. Do you find anything in this scene besides frivolous word-play and rather laborious trifling ? Note that its action repeats that of an earlier scene. Few serious modern dramatists would dare to venture a scene of such mere padding. What saved it for its Elizabethan audience ?

6. Why is Olivia made to declare her love ? How is the unpleasantness of this somewhat softened ?

III, 2.

1. Comment upon the splendid audacity and vigor of expression in 19–67. These lines have no languishing Victorian prettiness but they contain poetry of a high order — masculine, downright, dynamic. What sentences seem especially worthy of note ?

*2. Make a list of the second person pronouns in 1–12, noting by whom they are used and to whom they are addressed.

See Abbott's *Shakespearean Grammar*, articles 232–235. Give examples of the same phenomenon in other languages. What is the social status of Fabian?

III, 3.

1. Is this scene valuable in and for itself or for its dramatic function alone? What scenes are linked by it? Have we been in danger of forgetting Sebastian?
2. Compare Antonio's generosity here with his effusive affection earlier. Does it seem any more natural than the other?

III, 4.

1. What is the value of 5–6?
2. Where does Malvolio show a becoming modesty in 71–92? Do you think the poet shows extraordinary insight in the comment made by Malvolio upon Olivia's use of the word "fellow"?
3. Explain the frequent references to hell and devils in 93 *ff.*
4. With l. 137 compare III, 1, 65–66.
5. Comment upon the dramatic effect secured by 140–141. Compare *Julius Cæsar*, II, 1, 226–227, I, 2, 258–262, and III, 1, 111–116.
6. Viola's disguise wears very thin in 238 *ff.* Note especially 331–333. Has she enough at stake to warrant her in retaining it? How much would she gain and lose in declaring her sex at the present juncture? But the poet has two acts yet to write.
7. Is it easily believable that Antonio, who has seen Sebastian within the day, should take Viola for her brother? Where has the poet tried to prepare for this? Where, later, does he try to bolster it up? What very early Shakespearean comedy does the device recall? Would the awkwardness of the device be lessened or increased on the stage?
8. Comment upon "imagination," l. 409. Does it not seem that Viola has had all the evidence she could desire? Why does the poet keep her in suspense?

9. What leads Sir Toby to make the remark in 411–413? Note that the preceding speeches are in rhymed verse.
10. Why should Viola have imitated her brother? There is a delicate and easily overlooked touch of pathos in 414–418a.

IV, 1.

1. What very effective use is made here of the confusion between Sebastian and Viola?
2. Why is this second impending duel stopped?
3. Why does Olivia give such a lame excuse for her invitation in 58b–61a?
4. Why is it effective to make Sebastian yield so readily to her invitation?

IV, 2.

1. What is the stage setting of this scene? Compare III, 4. 148.
2. Where does the clown stand in talking with Malvolio? Why does not Malvolio overhear the comments of Sir Toby and Maria?
3. If what Maria says in 69–70 is true, what dramatic value has Feste's disguise?
4. Explain 106–109.
5. What is your feeling toward Malvolio at the end of this scene?
6. How does the song fit the occasion?

IV, 3.

1. Explain the boldness and the apparent suddenness of Olivia's demand in 24–28, in the light of her previous experience.
2. How does this demand of hers assist the poet in the complications yet to follow?
3. Why does Sebastian accept the situation so unquestioningly?

V, 1.

1. Is there any significance in the fact that Feste appears at the opening of each of the last three acts?

2. Paraphrase 54–62.

3. Show that Viola cannot be entirely sincere in 69–71 and
   95. Compare III, 4, 409–410. What hinders her from
   telling what she so strongly suspects? Note carefully
   the mood indicated in 256 ff. Do you like her less
   or more for this?

4. Why is Olivia's use of the name "Cæsario" in l, 109
   surprising and improbable? When has she had opportunity to learn her lover's real name, and thereby to
   untangle the whole complication before the present
   scene begins?

5. Comment fully upon l. 102. How does it fit into the
   time scheme you have made for the play?

6. Note the Duke's erudition in things amatory shown in
   120–123. Where have we seen this trait in him before?

7. Do you think 123–141 present a strong dramatic situation, without regard to the improbabilities upon which
   it is based?

8. Does it seem natural that Antonio should stand so
   long without speaking or being spoken to? Was not
   the Duke's concern with him sufficiently urgent to
   warrant instant attention? Does the poet allow us to
   forget Antonio so as not to mar the joyous effect of
   the comedy's final scene? What events finally crowd
   Antonio out of our minds altogether? What is done
   with his case?

9. With 252–255 compare II, 1, 19-20.

10. How is the Malvolio action dexterously drawn back to
    the center of the stage?

11. Discuss the tone of Malvolio's letter, 310 ff.

12. Does Fabian tell the exact truth in 363 ff.? Why?

13. When did the marriage mentioned in l. 372 occur?
    Why was it kept secret from Olivia? Has it been
    adequately prepared for? What evidence is there that
    Sir Toby married Maria because he was so hugely
    pleased with her plot against Malvolio?

14. Is it well to have the Malvolio action crowd out that
    of Viola at the end of the play? How might this effect
    be softened in action?

15. What unexpected element do you find in the character of Malvolio in 338-352?

16. What is the significance of the exit speech of Malvolio? Is it in the key of comedy? Considering that it is his last speech in the play, does it appear that Malvolio has profited by his lesson?

17. What evidences of haste do you find in this closing scene? Is there any action that is not completed? Is there any action that is not completed gracefully?

HAMLET

GENERAL QUESTIONS

1. How many stories or separate lines of interest do you find? In most of Shakespeare's plays the action revolves upon several pivots — there are several foci of interest. How and why does this play differ? Show in some detail how every bit of action is related to one central figure — that of the Lord Hamlet. Show that every other character is faced toward him and that every problem in the play is colored by his character and attitude.

2. What extraneous or unnecessary material do you find? Does it seem likely that Shakespeare added to the play from time to time after its completion? What technical faults do you discover in the construction?

3. Present evidence in favor of the view that the first three scenes of Act IV should be considered the last three scenes of Act III. Accepting this arrangement, outline briefly the material of each act.

4. Compare the play, as to length and construction, with *Macbeth*. Explain differences.

5. Which of the characters seem unmistakably English? How much is done to give a Danish flavor to characters and setting? Does the poet seem greatly concerned about this matter of "local color"? Compare his practice in other plays. Which of the characters seem Elizabethan? Is Hamlet or Laertes closer to the Elizabethan ideal?

6. Collect all evidence bearing upon the question of Hamlet's sanity. If you conclude that his madness was real — basing your opinion upon the text alone without regard to any critical comment — be prepared to say just what form his madness took and how long

it endured. If you conclude that his madness was assumed, be prepared to explain his manner, words, and actions on all occasions upon some tenable hypothesis. Do not think, as so many superficial readers and critics have done, that the whole question is settled by Hamlet's words in I, 5, 168 *ff.*, or by his assertions that he is sane. May this whole question, which has addled many weaker brains than Hamlet's, be, after all, largely a matter of definition? Show that it is dramatically and æsthetically necessary that Hamlet should be sane and normal at least in large part. Is a madman conceivable as protagonist of a real tragedy?

7. Collect all the evidence tending to show that Hamlet was capable of prompt, decisive action. Collect all evidence tending to show that he was so absorbed by the inner world of contemplation that he lost touch with and control of the outer world, consuming all his energy in thought. On which side does the evidence preponderate? But is it fairly strong and convincing on the other side also? Try to harmonize the two views.

8. Enumerate the occasions on which Hamlet determines upon instant action. What obstacle, real or imagined, prevents him in each instance?

9. Show the contrast, along many lines, between Hamlet and his environment. What are some of the more important character contrasts in the play?

10. Give as many illustrations as possible of the fact that Hamlet's mind dwells habitually upon the universal aspects of things and is not at its best in dealing with the individual and particular fact. Show that he realizes this weakness. Does this lack of mental balance fully explain his failure?

11. What weight should be given to the events preceding the action of the play — the death of Hamlet's father and the marriage of his mother — in explaining Hamlet's unfitness for action? In other words, do you agree with the opinion of A. C. Bradley that Hamlet's weakness is not inherent but only the temporary result of

what we might call "nervous shock"? If one accepts this view, he solves at once the quandary indicated in question 7. But is it characteristic of Shakespeare to base his tragic effects upon merely temporary and pathological states and conditions of mind? Does he not usually ground everything upon the bedrock of enduring character and does not the wealth and profundity of his effects depend largely upon his so doing? Professor Bradley's opinion makes Hamlet the victim of that blind Fate that rules in Greek tragedy, but Shakespeare seems to have remembered at all times the truth expressed in the Greek saying: "Character alone is Fate."

12. Show that each one of the deaths in the play is in some way related to Hamlet's weakness and failure. Nowhere does the poet render more perfectly than in this play the closely woven texture of life.

13. The *Tragedy of Hamlet* has held the stage, on the whole, better than any other of Shakespeare's plays. Its interest and appeal have increased steadily for three centuries. Is it somewhat better suited to the modern stage than to the Elizabethan? Why? In what ways does it seem better adapted to the modern mind than to the Elizabethan? What features of the play explain its undeniable popularity with the Elizabethan audience? Are we of to-day interested primarily in the same features?

14. Give some reasons for the general belief that this play marks the height of Shakespeare's achievement. Do you entirely agree with this belief? Give some reasons for ranking it lower, in certain particulars, than *King Lear*, than *Macbeth*, than *Othello*. But remember that such attempts to grade works of supreme excellence are of little value. In this case they serve their purpose if they show that while Shakespeare reached ultimate perfection nowhere, and, like a true romantic, seems scarcely to have sought it, the mountain which he climbed had more than one peak.

DETAILED QUESTIONS

I, 1.

1. What common knowledge is there between the four men present at the opening of the scene? How does it affect the manner and words of each?

2. What is the emotional tone and effect of these opening lines? To what elements is this effect due?

3. Show that in these lines the play is at once connected with past action. Do they also arouse strong curiosity regarding the future? Can you cite any other play in which these two important things are accomplished at one and the same time?

4. Do 1–69 set the key for the whole play? Explain. Do they, in general, provide what seems to you the best possible opening for the play?

5. Visualize the scene on the platform, with all the action contained in 1–69, and describe in detail.

6. How does the character of Horatio contrast with those of his associates? Are his associates differentiated in any way?

7. What dramatic effect is made by the skepticism of Horatio? What evidences are given in this scene of the scholarship of Horatio? In what ways does his character conform to the scholar type?

8. Explain l. 42. Compare *Much Ado*, II, 1, 264.

9. Comment upon l. 85. Is the poet writing solely from the point of view of the speaker or has he his Elizabethan audience also in mind in this line? Show that in other plays and in more important matters than the present one he often sacrifices realism to immediacy of appeal.

10. Show from this scene that no one has as yet suspected that the elder Hamlet met his death by foul play.

11. What is the meaning and etymology of " extravagant," l. 154, and of "probation," l. 156? Are they used in their derived English sense or in the sense they had in the language from which they come? What does

their use in this sense indicate in regard to the speaker?

12. What exposition in this scene? Is it cleverly introduced, so as to seem to spring naturally from the action?

I, 2.

1. Enumerate the various ways in which the speaker in 1–50 shows hypocrisy, diplomacy, and knowledge of men. Does he seem a man of personal and intellectual power? Point out one or two exhibitions of extraordinary cleverness in this speech. What single phrases have unusual strength and beauty? With l. 11 compare *Winter's Tale*, V, 2, 81–82.

2. How is Hamlet dressed in this scene? Make suggestions for the acting of his part. Does he suspect the king of the murder of his father? Is his present mood to be explained entirely by his natural sorrow for his father?

3. What is the etymology of "kind," l. 65? Explain the line.

4. What do we know of the queen from her first words? She utters profound truths as witlessly as a gramophone. Hamlet, in reply, cramps a world of meaning into five words.

5. Characterize Hamlet's replies to the king and queen. What is the double intention of 83b–84?

6. What is the precise nature of the king's attitude toward Hamlet? Why is he unwilling that Hamlet should return to Wittenberg? Why does Hamlet wish to return? What does this desire indicate regarding his character? Why does he yield so readily?

7. Comment fully upon the character and mood indicated in 129–159.

8. Read these lines over many times. Be prepared to render every nuance and shade of thought and feeling by the voice alone. This exercise is more important and should take more time than all the other questions on the scene together.

9. Compare the blank verse of this the first of Hamlet's

soliloquies with that of *Comedy of Errors*, II, 2, 112–
148. What essential differences do you find?

10. How long and how well has Hamlet known Horatio?
Compare 161 and 163 with III, 2, 59 *ff*. Is there any
evidence here of the close, long-standing friendship between the two which has so long served as a staple
article in Hamlet criticism? Where have the two met
before? Do they seem congenial? Or is Hamlet's
coldness here due to his distraught condition of mind?

11. What has led Hamlet to "doubt some foul play"?
Why does he suspect this before the others do?

12. What exposition in this scene? Is the greater part of
the necessary exposition now completed?

I, 3.

1. With 7–9 compare sonnet 99.

2. Comment closely upon the character indicated in 10–44.
Are these the words of a man truly wise or of one only
"worldly-wise"? Is the speaker pure of heart himself? Has he a belief that his sister is so? Would he
think it desirable that she should be so? What seems
to be his notion of the normal relations existing between
men and women?

*3. Where has the character of Laertes been formed? See
Ascham's *The Scholemaster* on the general subjects of
foreign travel and the "Italianate" Englishman. Show
the relation of the ideas there presented to Shakespeare's portrait of Laertes.

4. Comment closely upon the character shown in 55–81.
Several phrases and sentences from these lines have
passed, in the form of proverbs, into our common
speech, and this means that they must have wisdom of
some sort. Do they show the large and lordly wisdom
of the Sermon on the Mount or the grovelling, ignoble
wisdom of Franklin's *Poor Richard's Almanack*?

5. Illustrate from the present speech the fact that before
concluding that Shakespeare is expressing his own
thought in a given maxim or utterance, we should
always consider the source and the occasion of that

maxim or utterance. Shakespeare himself seems to have had little fondness for maxims and proverbs, but he puts them very frequently into the mouths of some characters. What kinds of characters, in the plays, are specially given to gnomic utterances? What kinds in life? Young or old? Educated or illiterate?

6. Where and how has the character of Polonius been formed? Is he at the height of his mental power or does he show signs of senile decay?

7. In what respects do these two companion speeches, 10-44 and 55-81, resemble each other? Does this seem natural and right? In what ways is Laertes like his father? How is Ophelia like both of them? In his treatment of this family Shakespeare has given his most careful and extended study of the influences of heredity and domestic environment. This line of interest is not obtruded, however. One discovers it only after close scrutiny. Acquaintance with it is of great importance in determining one's estimate of Ophelia.

8. Comment fully upon 85-89 and 136. Study all the intervening speeches of Ophelia. Granting the sweet docility with which she bows to the wills of brother and father — breaking her promise to the one almost as soon as made, it may be added, in order to obey the other — can you show that she has any strength, any conviction, any mind of her own? Shakespeare was interested in the question: Is this Ophelia a woman from whom a powerful but lonely and half-distracted man could renew his strength in the time of his greatest need? Is she that, or is she morally and intellectually nerveless? Is she something between these extremes?

9. It is clear, at least, that Ophelia is not the splendid, regal, large-minded woman who might have been a true mate to Hamlet. How, then, do you explain his "tenders of affection" to her?

10. Try to explain the main features of Ophelia's mind and character by reference to the state of affairs in her home.

11. Is it not natural to suppose that Polonius and Son would consider Hamlet a "good match"? What objections to him do they urge in speaking to Ophelia? What are their real objections? What is the importance of these objections in the rest of the play? Compare II, 1, 110 *ff.*

12. Though Polonius, quite fittingly, is the one who tells us that "brevity is the soul of wit," he is himself somewhat tedious. To show this, sum up each of his three long speeches in this scene in a single sentence.

I, 4.

1. What is the value of 8–22 in their application to the character and present state of mind of Hamlet? Does he feel in harmony with his environment?

2. How do 23–38 apply to the speaker himself? Have they any bearing upon the poet's purpose in the entire play?

3. Comment upon the style of 23–38. What does it indicate regarding the speaker's habit of thought?

4. Point out any single lines in 39–57 that seem to you particularly powerful and beautiful. Point out two lines in which the sound of the words is very delicately adjusted to the sense conveyed.

5. Visualize and describe the action of 39–85.

I, 5.

1. Can you see any good reason for marking a change of scene at this point? Is not the action continuous and the place almost the same as that of I, 4?

2. Paraphrase "eternal blazon," l. 21.

3. What comparison of great imaginative splendor do you find in 30–40?

4. Comment upon l. 40. Has Hamlet voiced his suspicions before?

5. What three injunctions are laid upon Hamlet by the Ghost? Does Hamlet remember each of them later and try to fulfill them all?

6. Show, from 92–112, that Hamlet thinks his mother had

some part in the murder of her first husband. Does he accuse her of this later?

7. Where has Hamlet learned the habit illustrated in 107–110a? Does the action seem appropriate at this time? How does it illustrate character? Does Hamlet think, like many another student, that he has accomplished something definite when he has "set it down" in his tables?

8. Explain the triviality of Hamlet's remarks in 116–164. Some critics think this is only a survival of low comedy material from the earlier Hamlet play, but even if it is, Shakespeare would scarcely have left it here unless he saw that it had dramatic value and suited his purposes.

9. What bearing have 169 ff. upon later events and your interpretation of them? Why should Hamlet think, so early as this, to give warning to his friends that he may act strangely? Has he a plan already in mind? If we suppose that he has, does not this argue an almost supernatural quickness of thought? Is it conceivable that he is already devising means by which he may delay action? Do you think the words "antic disposition" must necessarily refer to simulated madness?

10. What advance in action is made in this scene? Is all the necessary exposition now before us? Are we now ready for the main action of the play? What is the usual function of the first act in Shakespeare's tragedies?

11. What length of time elapses during the first act?

II, 1.

1. We have seen that neither Polonius nor Laertes trusts Ophelia. What more do we learn in this connection in 1–73? For what later action does this conference between Polonius and Reynaldo prepare the way?

2. How long after the action of I, 4, does Hamlet's visit to Ophelia occur? Has it any connection with any occurrences of that scene? Why does he go to see her? Can you explain the actions of Hamlet which Ophelia reports?

3. What feature of Hamlet's visit seems to have disturbed Ophelia most deeply, judging from 77–84? Compare III, 1, 161. Compare also *As You Like It*, III, 2, 398–401.

4. What construction does Polonius put upon Hamlet's action? Mark the willingness of Ophelia to agree with him. What is the importance of this opinion of his in the later action?

II, 2.

1. What earlier passage in the play is recalled by 1–39?

2. How many instances have we seen thus far in the play of weaker natures dominated and controlled for good or ill by stronger ones?

3. What light is thrown by l. 50 upon 1–39? Comment upon 56–57.

4. What part is played by Fortinbras and his soldiery in the action of the drama? Is it sufficient to justify the frequent mention of them?

5. How much trust does the king place in Polonius's declaration that Hamlet is mad with love of Ophelia? Why?

6. How many of the persons of the drama are completely taken in by Hamlet's counterfeit madness? Before which of these does he exhibit it with greatest glee? Why? Does Hamlet play the madman before any one consistently and all the time? What features of his mind make it very easy for Hamlet to deceive those about him in this way? What privileges and licenses very dear to him does Hamlet secure for himself by his simulated madness?

7. Is it perfectly clear and beyond question that Hamlet is only pretending madness in this scene?

8. What indications do you find in 170–223 that Hamlet knows of Polonius's plot against him? How could he have learned of it? More than once in the play he discovers intrigues against him by means which are left dark to us. This is a part of the silent testimony to his

superhuman intellectual subtlety. Ideas, bits of information, guesses, emotions, imaginations, suspicions, and
certitudes flash together in his mind from all the background of his experience and shape themselves instantly, it would seem, into orderly wholes, like the bits
of broken glass in a kaleidoscope. In the creation of
this mind Shakespeare gave us, as far as it was possible,
the reflex of his own.

9. Note that the dialogue between Hamlet and Polonius
is the first extended piece of prose in the play. Explain.

10. Find instances of delightful raillery in Hamlet's words
to Polonius. Find dramatic irony in Polonius's replies.

11. What indications are there that Hamlet knows Rosencrantz and Guildenstern are set to spy upon him? How
can he have learned this?

12. What do you think have been the previous relations
between Hamlet and the two spies? Was Goethe's
Wilhelm Meister right in thinking that Shakespeare
had these two hunt in a couple because one alone would
have been unnoticed, being of such light weight? What
is the bearing on this point of 33–34?

13. In what ways do 304–324 resemble Hamlet's soliloquies? Why is it perfectly natural that he should speak
on this occasion as though he were alone? Note that
this speech contains some of the noblest poetry uttered
by Hamlet in the play, and yet it is spoken chiefly with
the intent of making Rosencrantz and Guildenstern
think him mad. It succeeds. Why? If Hamlet has
only to speak to these normal, representative men as
he speaks habitually to himself in order to convince
them of his insanity, is there some real and important
sense in which he is actually insane? Is it clear that in
his ordinary intercourse with society, when he wishes to
appear sane, he must put a check upon his thought and
expression? Does this explain his delight in the game
he is playing at present?

*14. In what ways do 341–379 refer to theatrical con-
ditions in London at about the time *Hamlet* was writ- .

ten? See Furness *Variorum* notes. Is this sort of
reference to contemporary London affairs at all usual
with Shakespeare? Is it true to fact to represent English actors as performing in Denmark? Hamlet speaks
as though he had seen these players at Wittenberg.
Is this probable? See, if possible, Cohn's *Shakespeare
in Germany*.

15. How does all this talk about players and plays assist
the illusion of reality which it is always the dramatist's
desire to create? What does it tell us about Hamlet's
past life? Does it add anything to our notion of his
character? Does it advance the action?

16. What qualities in the lines about the fall of Troy does
Hamlet find praiseworthy? Do you think Shakespeare
is using Hamlet here as a mouthpiece for his own
opinions? Is it customary with him to speak his whole
thought through the mouth of any character? Is Shakespeare's dramatic writing excellent for the qualities
here praised? Do the specimen lines that follow seem
to deserve this praise?

17. What reasons does Hamlet give for employing the
device of the play in testing the king? Is he entirely
sincere with himself?

18. Can you give any explanation of the bombast and
fustian in the specimen lines? Is it not clear that Hamlet takes them seriously and really thinks them good?
When the players have left him, Hamlet speaks of
their performance with praise. Coleridge thought the
lines were actually good. They are in reality a sort of
parody of a passage in *Dido, Queen of Carthage*, supposed to have been written by Marlowe and Nash.
For one line of explanation, compare 577 *ff*. The poorer
the play, the more effective had to be the acting. A.
W. Schlegel had an interesting opinion that "to distinguish these lines as dramatic poetry in the play itself,
it was necessary that they should rise above its dignified poetry in the same proportion that the theatrical
elevation does above simple nature." Does this comment seem to hold good for the play within the play

in the following act? Does it hold good for that in *The Tempest*?

19. Into what divisions does this scene fall?

20. Show that a considerable space of time separates the action of Act I from that of Act II.

III, 1.

1. Why does Ophelia so easily consent to act as decoy to the man she loves?

2. Are 56–88 organic? That is, are they applicable to the situation of the speaker? Prove your point in detail. Might this great speech have been placed in any other part of the play as well as here?

3. Memorize these lines.

4. Compare this soliloquy with sonnet 66. Does it seem safe to draw any inference from the resemblance?

5. Explain the sudden change in Hamlet's manner in l. 103. How far does this changed manner persist?

6. Are Hamlet's words to Ophelia in 107 *ff.* in any way applicable to her? Explain. What leads him to speak so?

7. What is the effect of Ophelia's "At home, my lord" upon Hamlet? Why? For what reasons may we consider this line as marking the climax of the play?

8. What do 158–169 indicate regarding Ophelia's intellectual powers, character, and former attitude toward Hamlet? Does she see chiefly those things in Hamlet which her brother would have valued in himself or in another man? With 168a compare II, 1, 102. Does Ophelia misinterpret Hamlet's manner because of her feminine tendency to explain everything in terms of amatory passion or because she relies upon her father's opinion — or for both reasons?

9. Is the king convinced by Hamlet's show of madness? Compare 170 and 196. Why?

10. What appears to be the leading feature of Polonius's diplomacy? Give several illustrations.

III, 2.

1. Is Shakespeare speaking his own thought solely in 1–50? Or are these the words of one who is only a highly intelligent amateur? If the former supposition seems the more likely, give some reasons that may have led the poet to depart, in this instance, from his habit of professional reticence. Remember that throughout his public career Shakespeare's work as an actor must have absorbed more of his time and attention than his activity as a dramatist. Remember also his managerial position at the Globe Theater.

2. Sum up in a few words Hamlet's advice to the players. How much of it applies to dramatic writing as well as to acting? Comment fully upon the statement that the "purpose of playing . . . is to hold . . . the mirror up to nature." Is Hamlet arguing for what we understand as realism in acting?

3. Why does Hamlet choose just this time to bind himself closer to Horatio? Compare question 10, on I, 2. Judging from the character Hamlet gives to Horatio do you consider the latter a highly lovable person? Why does Hamlet seem so fond of him at the present juncture of events? Would he admire him so much under other conditions?

4. Is Hamlet right in his estimate of Horatio? What is the leading trait in Horatio's character, according to Hamlet? Note that Horatio provides the norm or standard by which we estimate the aberrations of Hamlet. This is his dramatic function. It is not easy to make such personifications of normality interesting in and for themselves.

5. What apparent fault is there in giving the argument of the play in dumb show, that is, in presenting the poisoning scene twice?

6. Discuss the literary quality of the play within the play. Why are the lines in rhymed verse? Is Schlegel's explanation of the bombast in the earlier specimen lines — quoted in question 18 on II, 2 — applicable here?

7. Where are the " dozen or sixteen lines " written by Hamlet for insertion in the play? Compare II, 2, 565–568. Be prepared to support your choice.

8. Comment upon l. 279. What inference do you draw from it?

9. Do Hamlet's high spirits in the rest of the scene arise from his demonstration of the king's guilt or from his delight in the complete success of the artistic means used in the demonstration?

10. With 282–285 compare *As You Like It*, II, 1, 45–63.

11. Comment upon the manner of Rosencrantz and Guildenstern in their talk with Hamlet. How do you explain the change since their first meeting?

12. Does it seem wise for the king and queen to show " choler " and "amazement" at anything Hamlet has done?

13. What is the meaning of " by and by," l. 400, in Shakespeare? Explain the change to the sense in which it is used to-day. Compare " presently."

14. With 393–399 compare V, 2, 95 *ff.*

15. Which of the three injunctions of the Ghost are recalled in 410 *ff.* ?

III, 3.

1. Where has the king shown contrition before? What advantage is gained in showing that he suffered some remorse? But how is the moral validity of his remorse almost entirely nullified?

2. What famous passage in Shakespeare is recalled by 43b–46a?

3. Estimate carefully the character and present mood of the speaker in 36–72. Is Shakespeare " fair " to Claudius? That is, is he careful to show the good with the bad and to give due weight to all the motives leading to evil action? Is Claudius still morally and spiritually alive?

4. Is Hamlet presented as Roman Catholic or Protestant in 72–96? Does the passage afford any clue to the religious beliefs of Shakespeare?

5. Is the reason here given by Hamlet for delaying revenge entirely sincere? In reality, why does he delay? Comment upon l. 96. How does it apply to Hamlet?

III, 4.

1. What irony in l. 4b? In l. 6? Note the moral obtuseness implied in the latter words. The queen intends to reprove Hamlet as she did when he was a child. The words are wonderfully natural and true.

2. In l. 6 the queen shows that her motherhood is of the lowest type. In 21–22a she shows that her womanhood is of the same sort by taking advantage of all its prerogatives while accepting none of its obligations. Show this fully. Is there any evidence in the text that Hamlet threatens her life? Why, then, does she cry out, endangering his life in so doing? What is there in Hamlet's manner and words to cause her to explode in this way? Compare carefully and comment upon 21–22a and 30a.

3. Compare and comment upon 26b and 32a. What makes Hamlet so prompt to strike here, although just before he could not?

4. Comment upon the supreme fitness and justice of the manner of Polonius's death. Who is really responsible for it?

5. Does it seem natural and right that Hamlet should make so little of the killing of Polonius?

6. Against what accusation is the queen bracing herself in 39–40a and 51b–52? Why is she here so bold and confident? Is it the boldness of real innocence? How does Hamlet beat down this guard?

7. Support from this scene alone your opinion as to whether the queen was innocent or guilty in the matter of her first husband's murder. The evidence on either side is intangible and elusive. Why, after all, does it matter little?

8. What action should accompany the speaking of 53–54?

9. Why does not the queen see or hear the ghost of her former husband?

10. How and when has Hamlet's purpose been "blunted"? Explain the reasons for the Ghost's appearance.
11. Comment upon l. 200a. Why does Hamlet wish to know whether his mother knows of it? How does he know of it himself? Cf. III, 1, 177, III, 3, 4, and IV, 3, 48b.

IV, 1.

1. Does it seem natural that a new act should begin here?
2. Does the queen do as Hamlet asks her to do in III, 4, 181 ff., in this scene? Comment upon l. 27b.
3. Comment upon the queen's characterization of Polonius.

IV, 3.

1. With 20–33 compare. V, 1, 218–239.
2. With 48–50 compare III, 4, 199–204. Are these passages inconsistent?
3. Give more than one reason why Hamlet is not sorry to start for England.
4. Judging from this scene, date the action of the play approximately.

IV, 4.

1. What justification is there for presenting Fortinbras and his army here, aside from the fact that it affords Hamlet occasion for another self-accusing soliloquy? Why is it important that we should be aware of the contrast between Hamlet and Fortinbras?

IV, 5.

1. Comment fully upon 17–20. How do these lines bear upon the question of the queen's complicity in the murder, or at least guilty knowledge of it?
2. Try to thread the maze of thoughts and emotions vaguely indicated in Ophelia's songs and speeches. Does she know how her father met his death? What ideas does her mind chiefly run upon? Would it appear that Ophelia has lost her mind because of some fearful strain that it has been subjected to or because

she had not much mind to lose? The poet's problem has been to make her fit to attract Hamlet yet too weak to hold him.

3. Explain the queen's meaning in 109–110. Of what or whom is she thinking? Compare l. 128c. To whom is she loyal, — husband or son?

4. What consideration mars the apparent nobility of 120–127? Is Claudius depending chiefly upon his divine right or upon his "Switzers"?

5. Note that the queen is present while 140–152 are spoken and must know well what the king intends, yet she makes no protest either here or later. Why does the king postpone further talk with Laertes in 202 *ff.*?

6. Comment upon the manner of Laertes throughout this scene. Granting him manliness, energy, and determination, what fault do you find in his manner? Does he remind you in any way of Polonius in these speeches? What fault does Hamlet find with it in V, 1, 277 *ff.*?

IV, 6.

1. Is there anything strange in the story Hamlet writes of the meeting with the pirate ship? Can you explain it? Does it seem natural that Hamlet should be the only one captured? Compare III, 4, 210. Why does Hamlet say, "They knew what they did"?

IV, 7.

1. With 18–21 compare IV, 3, 4–7. Does Hamlet seem the sort of man to win great popularity with the people? Compare III, 1, 158 *ff.*

2. Outline the method by which the king wins Laertes to his purpose.

3. Is it better that the suggestion of the poisoned foil should come from Laertes, as here, or from Claudius, as in the first quarto? Note that the suggestion of the poisoned cup comes from Claudius and that the speakers suggest the means of their own deaths.

4. What elements of beauty do you find in the report of Ophelia's death?

V, 1.

1. What is the æsthetic purpose of the low comedy? Distinguish the two clowns. Comment upon the elaborate logical processes of the first clown. Where has he caught this habit or manner? Compare Dogberry.

2. Does Hamlet remind you of Jaques in any way in this scene?

3. What is the dramatic value of the clown's statement that Hamlet was "sent into England"?

4. What is the age of Hamlet? Does this agree with other indications and with your feeling? Compare I, 3, 124.

5. Comment upon Laertes' manner in his mourning. What false note does Hamlet catch in it? Explain Hamlet's bombast in 298 *ff*. Compare V, 2, 79–80a.

6. How does this scene advance the action and prepare for later events? What important character contrast does it emphasize? Comment upon the wide emotional range of the scene.

V, 2.

1. Comment upon 7b–11a as an illustration of Hamlet's character. Is there anything surprising in this praise of rashness and indiscretion? Where has this trait been illustrated before? How does its expression here prepare for the closing events of the play?

2. What is the purpose of 1–62? Why is it necessary that we should know of the events here related? With these events in mind, what do you think of the view that Hamlet was temperamentally unfit for action and of the view that he had an invincible aversion to violence and bloodshed? Compare III, 4, 202 *ff*. and explain Hamlet's evident delight in the remembrance of these events.

3. Do you think that Rosencrantz and Guildenstern got simple justice? Is it certain that they knew the contents of the king's letter to England? But is this the whole question?

4. Explain 77–78a. What is the dramatic value of this parallelism and how far does it extend? What is the

value for future events of Hamlet's desire to conciliate Laertes ?

5. Paraphrase 108–129. What is Hamlet's purpose in his reply ? Show, by comparison with other passages in which there is no suggestion of parody, that Shakespeare is here burlesquing his own style.

6. Paraphrase 195–202. Is this passage of "Shakespearese" any less difficult and affected in style than 108–129, which is obviously a parody of Euphuistic or Arcadian speech ?

7. What is the dramatic value of 220–235 ? Show that Hamlet expects more than a mere fencing match — that, as always, he sees the trap before walking into it.

8. Discuss the sincerity of 237–255a. Compare 215–216. Note the black treachery of Laertes' reply and contrast his desire to keep his honor unsmirched before the world. What hereditary trait here ?

9. Comment upon the merits of 291–342 as stage spectacle.

10. Is the king's punishment adequate ? Show that the final seal is set upon Hamlet's failure in this scene, the scene in which he accomplishes his task. In speaking of Hamlet's failure, do we refer to the injunctions laid upon him by the Ghost or to the fact that he has not commanded and exerted his full resources as a man ? How much part has "poetic justice" in this final closing of accounts and how much has mere blind chance ? Does the close of the play illustrate the truth of 10–11a?

11. Paraphrase and explain the full meaning of 355–360a. Try to express a part, at least, of Hamlet's meaning in his last, unforgettable words, "The rest is silence."

12. What is the dramatic purpose and value of Fortinbras' entrance and of Hamlet's delegation of the throne to him ? Compare the last lines of *King Lear* and the close of *Macbeth*. How has this been prepared for ? In what ways is Fortinbras really a better man for the throne than Hamlet ?

13. Comment upon the solemn grandeur of the closing tableau.

OTHELLO

GENERAL QUESTIONS

1. Outline the plot. With what incident does the action start? Where is the climax of the play? Why does it occur so late? In other words, why is the "rising action" so much longer than the "falling action"? Does any single character originate and control the action?

*2. What length of time actually elapses during the action that is shown and the intervals indicated in the text? Is there any disparity between this actual time and the time that is suggested to the imagination? Point out the devices by which the poet builds up an illusion of a lapse of time different from the actual one. What is the purpose of this double time scheme?

3. Enumerate all the important ways in which Othello is commended to our sympathy, respect, and admiration. Why is this done with such extreme care and in so many different ways? Does the poet consider such elaborate recommendation necessary for his other tragic heroes — say Coriolanus and Macbeth? How far through the play does the effect of this extend?

4. Discuss, in general, Othello's nobility. Quite apart from the closing events of his life, do you find any elements of pathos in his character and experience? Gather all hints as to what he has been in the past. What are his most serious limitations in mind and knowledge? Are these limitations, like those of Coriolanus, Lear, and Macbeth, derogatory to his character or are they, like those of Romeo, Brutus, and Hamlet, rather the "defects of his qualities"? What is the bearing of this upon the total effect of the play?

*5. Show in detail that Iago's character is designed with

extreme nicety for just the part that he is to play. A careful study of this matter may illumine some of the darker secrets of the poet's creative methods. It may help toward a solution of the interesting question as to whether he started to work with several fixed and invariable characters or whether he chose only one or two such fixed characters and made all the others fit into them.

6. Pleasure, according to Herbert Spencer, is only the "normal functioning of an organ in an act." Try to explain Iago's intrigue from this point of view. What is the nature of Iago's power? Can it be shown that the wickedness of this most thoroughly evil man ever imagined is due to the fact that he lives solely in the realm of intellect?

7. What are the motives of Iago's action? Hatred of virtue, nobility, worth, and of those who show these qualities? Desire for revenge? Jealousy? Lust? Greed? Longing for a thorough trial of his powers? Cite all passages bearing upon the point and make your decision, remembering that Iago prefers falsehood to honesty even in his soliloquies. Is it necessary to suppose that he himself knew his motives clearly and fully?

8. Collect all passages bearing upon the following questions: Is Othello naturally and inherently a jealous man? Can it be proved that he is jealous at any point in the play? As a supreme test, consider carefully V, 2, 1–83. Remembering the great difference between what we know and what Othello knows of Iago, do you think that Othello's final conviction of his wife's guilt argues stupidity, credulity or a predisposition to jealousy on his part?

9. Does Othello take Desdemona's life in anger, in a fit of jealousy, to protect and avenge his wounded honor, or as an act of disinterested judgment upon her?

10. Show that Othello and Desdemona come to grief because of their nobility and that they could scarcely have acted in any way other than that here shown

without inconsistency or dishonor. For example, is it not greatly to their credit that they could not conceive such duplicity as that of Iago ?

11. State very carefully the effect of the play upon you after a rapid reading. Few plays suffer more in entire impressionistic effect from the sort of analysis here outlined, but it is hoped that this analysis will show that the impressionistic effect of the whole is not all that is to be sought in a great work of art, although it is unquestionably the greater part. No other tragedy of Shakespeare's is so well fitted to the stage. One does not know the play's gigantic power until he has seen it adequately performed.

12. Compare this play in any ways that seem to you important with *Hamlet*, *Macbeth*, and *King Lear*.

DETAILED QUESTIONS

I, 1.

1. What is the foundation and cause of the friendship between Iago and Roderigo?

2. Is Roderigo in any sense a bad man? What is his fault?

3. What evidences of Othello's importance do you find in 1–33?

4. Characterize Cassio, basing your judgment entirely upon 18–31. It is evident that in order to derive the real Cassio from this description we should have to subtract a large admixture of Iago. Is this true of Iago's pronouncements in general? Is he incapable of seeing men and events as they really are?

5. What character does Iago give himself in 41–65? Does he think this is his true character?

6. Why does Iago feel so free to reveal his character and motives to Roderigo? What important dramatic purpose is served by this? Show that Roderigo's character was designed to serve this purpose. Do you think Iago is making sport of Roderigo in 1–80?

7. With l. 143 and l. 172 compare I, 2, 63, *ff*. Comment.

8. Collect the oaths of Iago in this scene. What is their nature? Does Iago use them and choose them with design?

9. What exposition in this scene? What other purposes does the scene serve?

I, 2.

1. How does Iago's manner and bearing toward Othello differ from his manner and bearing toward Roderigo? How has he gained Roderigo's confidence? How that of Othello?

2. Point out evidences of poise and self-confidence in Othello in 1–32.

3. With 48–52 compare III, 3, 71–72.

4. Explain Iago's motive in l. 58.

5. Comment upon l. 59. Supreme self-possession speaks in the very rhythm of the words.

6. What exposition in this scene? State carefully the purpose of the first two scenes. Discuss Dr. Johnson's opinion that the play would have been improved by the elimination of these scenes and the mere narration of their action.

7. How much needs to be added to the characters of Othello and Desdemona as presented thus far in order to make a full and rounded picture?

8. What is the importance for the play of Iago's control of Roderigo? What preparation for later events do you find in the manner in which that control has been gained?

I, 3.

1. Do 1–47 advance the action? What purpose do they serve?

*2. Othello is not a Venetian. Then why is he employed on such a mission as that mentioned in 48–49? What famous soldiers were employed in much the same way by other Italian cities?

3. Considering the importance of the state business in

progress, do you think the interruption of it in 52–220 realistic and convincing?

4. Comment upon the character shown in 76–94. Note the great beauty and power of this and of Othello's next long speech.

5. Comment upon l. 121. Compare l. 285 and l. 295.

6. Is there any change in your attitude toward Brabantio as the scene proceeds?

7. What is the special significance, in view of later events, of 293–294?

8. Explain the change to prose in l. 302.

9. What characterization do you find in 321–337? Comment upon the stress Iago gives to strength of will. Why is his opinion of love important and significant?

10. Explain the many repetitions of "put money in thy purse" in 338–368.

11. Coleridge explains 389–410 as the "motive hunting of a motiveless malignity." D. N. Snider thinks the motives here expressed are sincere. Support either opinion.

II, 1.

1. Note the successive stages of suspense regarding Othello's safety. What is the value of this suspense? How does it affect our attitude toward Othello?

2. Is Montano really glad that Othello is coming? Why? How does his attitude toward Othello help the characterization of the latter?

3. What is the dramatic value of Cassio's praise of Desdemona?

4. Coleridge says: "Iago's answers are the sneers that a proud, bad intellect feels toward women and expresses to a wife." Contrast Cassio's attitude toward women with Iago's.

5. Characterize Iago's talk about women. What is his age? Compare I, 3, 312.

6. Does Shakespeare seem to think that a man's attitude toward women is indicative of his character in general? Illustrate from *Julius Cæsar*. Of course, better men than Iago have held his opinions about women —

Strindberg, for example, and Schopenhauer, and Otto
Weininger. What seems to be Shakespeare's attitude,
judging from the mouth into which he puts these opinions ?

7. With 295 *ff.* compare I, 3, 392 *ff.* What inference do
you draw ?

II, 3.

1. Explain the insistence upon the idea expressed in 6b.
2. By what means does Iago persuade Cassio to drink ?
3. Show that Iago's song, 71–75, is suited both in sound
and sense to the singer. But is Iago really a lover of
drink ?
4. Compare 78–81 with *Hamlet*, I, 4, 8–32. Comment.
What is the value of Iago's saying, "I learned it in
· England " ?
5. Does it seem natural that Iago should speak in praise
of wine ?
6. Explain the story told by Iago in 225–239. Point out
the matchless cunning and superb daring of it all.
7. Are Cassio's words against wine, 282–284, often quoted
by advocates of prohibition, to be taken as an expression of Shakespeare's own thought on the subject?
Why ? Compare 313–315 and *II Henry IV*, IV, 3,
92–135.
*8. Comment upon the extensive use of the soliloquy in de-
veloping the character of Iago. Does it seem that in
his maturer work Shakespeare employs the soliloquy
chiefly for the elucidation of difficult and complicated
material, either in the way of character or in that of
action ? What additional reason for its use can you see
in the case of Iago ? What characters in Shakespeare's
plays are especially given to the soliloquy ? What characters soliloquize scarcely at all ? Why is this con-
venient device so seldom used to-day in dramatic
writing ?
9. Comment upon l. 385. What sort of pleasure does Iago
take in the plot he is weaving ?
10. Outline the intrigue of Iago up to the point it has

reached by the end of Act II. Explain each detail of his action as far as possible.

11. Comment upon l. 394. Why should Iago fear delay? Why does he drive the action at such a furious pace?

III, 1.

1. What is the dramatic effect of Cassio's determination to speak personally with Desdemona? That is, what effect is it calculated to have upon the audience?

2. Does it seem that Emilia is in league with her husband here?

III, 3.

1. Discuss the sincerity of 3–4. Where has Desdemona acquired the opinion expressed in l. 5a? Notice that the source of the opinion is such as to make it almost an article of religion with her.

2. What is the effect upon the audience of 22b–26? Point out dramatic irony in 26–28.

3. Why does not Cassio stay and what does he mean in saying that he is "unfit for his own purposes"? Does the important dramatic accident which occurs in 29–35 seem quite natural and unforced?

4. In what sense and degree is it true to say that the real action and conflict of the play begin with l. 35? Why do they begin so late? In most of Shakespeare's tragedies do we not look for the climax of the action at about this point?

5. What is the effect of Othello's short sentences in 40–59? Do you think the poet treats Othello's first touch of suspicion and its swift passing with perfect precision and restraint? The present passage has an important bearing upon the question as to whether Othello was of a naturally jealous disposition. What is the indication here?

6. What is the effect upon Othello of 76b–83a, just after he has granted his wife's request? Might he not well say with the queen in *Hamlet*, "The lady protests too much, methinks"? Show that throughout these crucial

moments Desdemona acts, quite innocently, in just the wrong way.

7. Infer the main features of Iago's plan of action from 94–95.

8. Why does Othello ask just the question in l. 103a of Iago? Into what two classes does Othello seem to divide men? Does Iago seem to have a larger number of pigeon holes?

9. Does not l. 119 express the exact truth about Iago? Comment.

10. Note that 155–161 constitute almost the only extended passage that is well known and frequently quoted from this play. What comment should be made upon the fact that they are spoken by the deepest-dyed villain in Shakespeare's theater? Should this not teach us caution in accepting every "wise saw and modern instance" in the plays as an expression of the poet's whole thought on the given subject? Yet it is clear, of course, that in this passage Iago speaks, with diabolical ingenuity, what he knows would be Othello's own noble thought on the subject of personal honor. Iago knows, as the devils do, what goodness is. His hypocrisy, here and everywhere except at the very end, is the grudging homage which he pays to virtue.

11. Show that Iago has arrived at the truth expressed in 155–161 during the process of his thought about the plot against Othello. Show that this truth may be considered as the foundation of that plot. Would Iago have spoken thus to Roderigo?

12. Upon what weakness in Othello is Iago playing in 163–164? Note the rejoinder.

13. What characteristic of Othello is indicated in 179b–180a?

14. Do you find any special strength and ingenuity in the stroke made by Iago in 200–204?

15. How is Desdemona's innocence pathetically and powerfully shown in l. 285?

16. Comment upon the dramatic accident noted in l. 287 and the stage direction. To what sort of feeling on the

part of Desdemona is this accident immediately due? How does it happen that she leaves the handkerchief?

17. Infer from 295–320 the nature of the relations between Iago and his wife.

18. Explain l. 329b. What is the secret of the great poetic beauty of 330–333a and 347b–357? Memorize the latter group of lines.

19. Why does Othello bid farewell to the "pomp and circumstance of glorious war"?

III, 4.

1. Compare the clown here presented with any other of the clowns and fools of Shakespeare that you know. Explain important differences on the ground that the poet wished to have the present play make a peculiar effect and calculated all details accordingly.

2. What do 55–68 and 69–75 add to your knowledge of Othello's past history and his resultant present character? What other value have these speeches? Do you think Othello is telling what he considers the truth about the history of the handkerchief?

3. Comment upon the lie told by Desdemona in 83 *ff*. Or is it a lie? What are its results?

4. Does the reason given by Cassio in 188–191 seem adequate? Comment.

5. What is the value of this scene between Cassio and Bianca, both for what is past and for what is to come?

IV, 1.

1. Criticize 46–48. Does it seem probable that Iago would speak thus? Why?

2. What is the meaning of "unbookish jealousy" in l. 102? Does the phrase fit the facts of the case?

3. Comment upon the entrance of Bianca after l. 149. How many dramatic accidents have we had thus far? Are they all slight and seemingly unimportant? Do they all tend in the same direction? That is, do they all favor Iago?

4. Comment upon Theobald's stage direction, "striking her," l. 251. Do you think it is probably correct?

IV, 2.

1. Comment upon the admirable stroke of characterization in 125–127.

IV, 3.

1. What is the source of the pathos in 28–54?
2. What is the probable purpose of Emilia in 87–104? Is it an unusual doctrine that she enunciates? Perhaps we should note again that there is no reason for supposing that the poet spoke his own thought through such mouthpieces as Iago and his wife. Emilia has reason, if any woman has ever had, to think ill of husbands, but this is not equivalent to saying that she is a good and an unbiased judge.

V, 1.

1. Which of the reasons Iago gives for killing Cassio seems nearest his real reason?
2. What is the immediate effect upon Othello of the wounding of Cassio?
3. What are Iago's reasons for killing Roderigo?
4. Comment fully upon the effect of this scene and upon the means by which it is secured.

V, 2.

1. What is the full meaning of l. 1? Of l. 7?
2. Explain "This sorrow 's heavenly," l. 21b.
3. What elements of strength, beauty, pathos, do you find in 1–22?
4. In this speech, and throughout the scene, collect as many passages as possible in which hate struggles with great tenderness. Which is the closer in its specific application to Desdemona — Othello's hate or his tenderness? Which is the more generalized?
5. Do you think the poet chose wisely in having Desdemona waken? What do her words add to our knowl-

edge of her feeling and thought? Does the colloquy add at all to our knowledge of Othello and sympathy for him?

6. Comment fully upon Desdemona's words and manner here. Despite, or rather because of their utter simplicity, these words are as thrilling as any Shakespeare ever wrote.

7. What two interpretations might be put upon l. 76? Which of the two does Othello seize upon? What is the result? Show that the immediate cause of Desdemona's death, like the causes of all her woes, is her higher nature, her kindliness, and, in the best sense of a long-suffering word, her sweetness.

8. Comment upon the dramatic accident in the time at which Emilia knocks at the door.

9. Compare the effect of this knocking at the door with the knocking at the gate in Macbeth. What have the two incidents in common, showing that the poet must have had a desired effect clearly in mind in both instances?

10. There is perhaps a pitch beyond which pathos may not pass and remain tolerable. Do you think that 124–125 come near the limit? There is only one line in Shakespeare — *King Lear*, V, 3, 274 — that transcends in pathos these words that Desdemona's heroic spirit struggles back through the dark to speak in defense of her lord.

11. By what means is this scene saved from the melodramatic tone which the events it contains tend so strongly to give it? Note especially the style of 23–83. There is no better illustration of the virtues of restraint and simplicity — qualities which Shakespeare could command upon occasion.

12. Outline the movement of Emilia's thought from 126 to 155. Compare her speeches after l. 155 with her earlier speeches in the play. What is the difference and how is it caused? Has the change been prepared for? Compare Emilia's treatment of Iago in 169 *ff.* with that in III, 3, 300 *ff.* Explain the difference.

13. Show that Othello has never thought of the killing of

his wife as a murder. Does this explain his lame defense before Emilia?

14. How does the killing of Emilia help the play?

15. With 243b–246a compare III, 3, 347–357.

16. Comment upon the manner of Othello's death. Does it
seem to you merely theatrical or natural, even inevitable?

KING LEAR

GENERAL QUESTIONS

1. Enumerate the actions of the play. Show their interconnections. Where do they run parallel and what contrasts do they present?

2. Into what three or four main groups may the persons of the drama be divided, according to character? Leading characteristic of each group? What characters oscillate between groups or pass from one to another?

3. Does this radical distinction between groups seem artificial or natural? What early form of English drama does it recall? What is its purpose? Is this a form and a purpose in which Shakespeare frequently worked? Why?

*4. Draw a simple diagram that will show the rise, culmination, decline, and ruin of the hero's power, with their relative durations. What is peculiar about the structure of this play? How is this peculiarity justified by the nature of the poet's problem? Draw a similar diagram for *Macbeth*. Deduce from these diagrams themselves as much as possible as to the nature of the tragedies they symbolize and the nature of the emotions they awaken, — whether chiefly sustained admiration, as in *Julius Cæsar*, admiration mingled with dislike, as in *Coriolanus*, love and fear, as in *Romeo and Juliet*, love and admiration intensified by our sense of the hero's fatal weakness, as in *Othello* and *Hamlet*, or simply great pity and an overpowering sense of inevitable, inscrutable Fate.

5. Comment upon the poet's daring in resting the whole tragedy upon a rather sordid family quarrel. Does this weaken or strengthen the pathos of the king's struggle? What facts make it certain that Shakespeare intended this play to symbolize the ancient, never-ending tragedy

of the two generations, or, as Tourgeniev phrased it, of *Fathers and Sons?*

6. Show that the poet does not wish us to sympathize exclusively with either side in this struggle but wants to make us see that the struggle is due to a universal law of nature that over-rides human hearts. Make out as good a case as you can for Goneril and Regan and for Edmund. What can be said against the greatly overpraised Cordelia? Wherein is the king clearly in the wrong? What is the source of our pity for him?

7. Discuss fully the function and character of the fool. Of Kent.

8. What differences do you find between Goneril and Regan? Compare their villainy, as to its motives, with that of Edmund. Compare their plot, a woman's plot, with Edmund's. Does it seem correct to say that Shakespeare's worst women sound greater depths of vileness than his worst men? Do the two sisters impress you as real, human, convincing? Does the contrast between them and Cordelia seem natural? Why does Shakespeare care less here than elsewhere about matters of verisimilitude?

9. What features of this play render an adequate stage presentation impossible? Why is it the supreme manifestation of Shakespeare's genius as poet but not of his genius as a writer for the stage? Why is it the fittest of all his plays for musical interpretation?

10. Professor A. C. Bradley says that the theme of this play is the redemption of a selfish old man through love and suffering. Does this seem adequate? What seems to be Shakespeare's solution, supposing that he had one, of the mystery of evil and pain?

DETAILED QUESTIONS

I, 1.

1. Should we attribute the evil in Edmund's nature to the actual conditions of his birth or to his father's attitude toward those conditions?

2. Was the formal partition of the kingdom in this scene the first indication to Lear's followers of his intention? Compare 3–7. Also l. 197.

3. What is the dramatic value of this? How does it link the action of the play with past time? What bearing has it upon 53–54?

4. Comment fully, both in praise and blame, upon Cordelia's answer. It does not follow from the fact that her sisters are inhumanly evil that Cordelia must be superhumanly good or anything like the epitome of all the feminine virtues that her admirers have made her out to be. She takes a rather stupid pride in her bluntness and she has not yet learned that the truth may be so baldly spoken as to make the effect of a lie. In this she is like Kent. But what can be said in extenuation?

5. Is Kent arguing, in 123 *ff.*, for Cordelia's good or for Lear's?

6. Is there in Lear's treatment of Kent any partial reason or justification for the later treatment of Lear by Goneril and Regan?

7. Why does Kent accept so calmly the sentence laid upon him by the abdicating king? Why does he not appeal to the new powers of the realm?

8. What is the attitude of Goneril and Regan toward Lear exhibited at the end of the scene? In what ways are they really superior to him?

I, 2.

1. Has Edmund's soliloquy the ring of sincerity? Does he probe to the rock bottom of his motives? Compare the motive-hunting soliloquies of Iago.

2. Comment upon the ease with which Gloucester is deceived.

3. What is the dramatic value of Gloucester's superstition and of Edmund's disgust at it?

I, 4.

1. What is the fool's attitude toward Cordelia, as indicated in this scene? In what relation does he stand

to Lear's own heart and thought? Why does he speak so constantly of Cordelia?

2. What inference do you draw from 295–296 and 312? Also from the words between Albany and Goneril at the end of the scene?

I, 5.

1. What is the motive of the fool's talk in this scene?
2. Find indications in Act I that Shakespeare thought of Lear as a pagan. What is the approximate date of the action? What, presumably, was Lear's religion? Do these matters in any way influence the poetic effect of the play? Is the play so largely symbolical and poetic as to be independent of time or place?
3. What is your feeling toward Lear at the end of Act I? What is the great lesson he has to learn?

II, 1.

1. Does the credulity of Edgar and Gloucester seem probable?
2. What qualities of Edmund's mind and character win him success here?
3. How does this scene illustrate the saying that "the children of darkness are wiser in their generation than the children of light"?
4. Why does Edgar display so much less quickness of wit here than he shows later in the play?
5. Show in detail that Shakespeare is entirely fair to Edmund, as he has been to the wicked sisters and as he is with even Iago, revealing the good with the bad. What admirable intellectual qualities, lacking in Edgar, relieve to some extent his moral baseness?
6. Do you think Gloucester's feeling adequate, at what he considers the villainy and treachery of Edgar? Have we been prepared for this emotional shallowness on his part?
7. Why was it dramatically necessary that the sorrow and anger of Gloucester should be somewhat wan and weak?

8. What parallelism do you find, up to and including the present scene, between the stories of Gloucester and Lear?

9. Explain the exact meaning of "natural" in l. 86 and of "from" in l. 126.

10. Why has Regan gone to visit Gloucester?

II, 2.

1. How does Kent betray his birth and breeding in the quarrel with Oswald?

2. Does Kent's conduct in this quarrel increase your confidence in his ability to serve Lear skillfully as well as faithfully? Why?

3. Do 101b–106 seem a just and apt characterization of Kent in both his strength and his weakness? How closely do they apply to Cordelia? Does the poet expect us to sympathize wholly with either of these two, or is this "saucy roughness" treated as an ugly fault which defeats its own ends? Note that it is a fault of manner only, but that it plays quite as important a part in precipitating the tragedy as does the moral turpitude of the sisters and of Edmund. Faults of manner are usually less easily forgiven than moral baseness. Kent and Cordelia suggest a reason.

II, 4.

1. Comment closely upon the function of the fool throughout this scene.

2. Find evidences of increasing patience in Lear.

3. What evidence do you find that Lear has not yet learned the great lesson that love is not to be tested by external things?

4. Outline the steady increase in emotional intensity throughout the scene.

5. What is the significance of the stage direction, "Storm and tempest," at l. 286? How long does the storm continue? What part of the action of the play elapses during the continuance of the storm? What is the symbolic purpose?

III, 1.

1. Compare l. 3 with I, 1, 183. Inference as to Kent's attitude toward Lear?

2. Point out, in 4–15, words that give a key to the mean ing of the storm scenes generally.

3. Do you find an inconsistency, or at least a straining, in the time scheme in Kent's announcement of the land ing of the French at Dover under Cordelia? Compare I, 4, 317. If there seems to be a double time scheme, explain its purpose and necessity. Compare *Othello*.

4. Why does the gentleman desire further talk with Kent?

5. Is Kent's direction, 52–55, followed out later?

III, 2.

1. How do the fool's speeches in the first 36 lines bear upon Lear's condition of mind and the causes of that condition?

2. Is this mere cruelty on the fool's part? Is there any doubt of the fool's affection for the king or of his de sire to serve him as best he can? What effect have his words upon the king?

3. Does the constant presence of the fool with Lear during the storm scenes add in any way to the pathos of the situation?

4. Point out one line of intense pathos in the first 36 lines. What is the cause of this pathos? Has this note been struck before in Lear's speeches?

*5. Characterize the speeches of Lear in this scene, espe cially as to power of poetic expression, imagination, intensity. Compare them closely with his speeches in II, 4, which are equally admirable in another way. It is important to remember that the great dramatic poet speaks not with one but with many voices. Each of Shakespeare's major characters has a style of his own. Compare Lear, in this matter of poetic power, with Romeo, Othello, Hamlet, Macbeth, Coriolanus. Each of these is a consummate master of speech, but each one voices his genius in a style peculiar to him-self. Differentiate these styles as precisely as possible.

6. Count the references to the storm in this scene. Note especially 42–49. If the play had been written for the modern stage, would there need to be so many? Why?

7. How well and how long does Lear keep the resolve, evidently sincere, made in l. 37? Is he really learning patience? What does he mean by, "I will say noth-ing"?

8. Is there evidence of radical change in Lear in the speech beginning with l. 49 and in the next speech of his? Compare also III, 4, 28 *ff*.

9. After reading as far as l. 59, re-read, from the begin-ning of the scene, all of Lear's speeches, consecutively. Do you find a logical continuity of thought? Do his second and third speeches seem in any way dependent upon the intervening words of Kent and the fool, or is he self-absorbed?

10. What is the connection of 59b–60a with what pre-cedes?

11. The song that closes *Twelfth Night* has been denied to Shakespeare. Compare the song of the fool, 74 *ff*. Is this conclusive either way?

12. Does the fool's "prophecy" fit the situation in any way?

III, 3.

1. What motives actuate Gloucester in siding with Lear?

III, 4.

1. What defects are there in the storm scenes as designed for stage presentation? Do these defects obtain equally for the reader?

2. Visualize and describe the scene before the hovel.

3. Compare 19 *ff*. with III, 2, 37.

4. Lines 28–36 are among the sublimest things in Shake-speare. Memorize them and be able to interpret each shade of meaning and emotion in reciting them.

5. Note that Lear thinks this speech a prayer. Why?

Is it really so in any sense ? Why does he think he can sleep after it ? What radical spiritual change has he undergone ?

6. What accident mades sleep impossible and so drags Lear over the brink into madness ? What is the immediate cause of his madness ? What bearing has this upon the interweaving of the two plots that compose the play ?

7. Where do you find the first certain signs that Lear is mad ?

8. Characterize the three kinds of insanity presented in this scene.

9. It has been fairly well established that exhibitions of simulated insanity were received by Elizabethan audiences as comic material. Do you think Shakespeare intended this scene to be so received in even the slightest degree, or did he wish to make an effect of unrelieved pathos and tragedy ?

*10. Compare Lear's speech, 105 *ff.*, with what you know or can learn of Carlyle's "Philosophy of Clothes" expounded in *Sartor Resartus*.

11. Express in your own words what Lear means by "unaccommodated man."

12. What is the dramatic and ethical fitness in the fact that this discovery about "unaccommodated man" is made by Lear ? How is it in harmony with the mediæval idea of tragedy ? Compare *The Canterbury Tales*, Group B, ll. 3163–67.

13. When did Kent speak the words ascribed to him by Gloucester in 168–169 ?

14. Explain the substitution of "British" for "English" in l. 189.

15. In how far does the tragedy of Gloucester parallel that of Lear in this scene ?

16. How is Gloucester's reaction like Lear's ? How unlike ?

III, 5.

1. Cornwall may be said to be only protecting his own interests in his persecution of Gloucester, whom he

thinks a traitor. But how is his action made perfectly
dastardly in the first line of the scene ?

III, 6.

1. Do 5–6 recall any of the words of Lear ?
2. Explain 16–17. Compare IV, 6, 190–191.
3. Read consecutively all the speeches of Lear in this
   scene. Have they any relation to what is said to him
   or done about him ? Are they logical and connected in
   themselves ? How much of Lear's insanity might be explained as intense and extreme self-absorption and pre-
   occupation with his own troubles?
4. Comment fully upon l. 92, the last words spoken by the
   fool in the play. What is their real meaning? What probably becomes of the fool ? What pathos do you feel in
   the fact that these are the first and the last words in
   which the fool speaks of himself ?
5. What evidence is in favor of the view that the parts of
   Cordelia and the fool were originally designed for and
   taken by the same actor ?
6. How should the part of the fool be acted after l. 92?
7. Some have thought that 109–122 were not written by
   Shakespeare. They are not in the *First Folio*. Do you
   see anything to support this opinion ? Could the words
   "he childed as I fathered" have been written by one
   who had not clearly in mind the parallels, contrasts, and
   interrelations of the two plots ? Do you find other lines
   and phrases that seem certainly Shakespeare's? What
   dramatic purpose do the lines serve ?

III, 7.

1. What people of the play are gathered at or near Gloucester's house at the opening of this scene ?
2. What dramatic purpose does this gathering serve ?
*3. By what movements and occurrences suggested in Acts
   I and II have they been so gathered ? Give details and
   line references.
4. Have you a clear idea where the Duke of Albany's castle
   is ? Cornwall's ? Gloucester's ? Lear's ? Had Shake-

speare? What is the poetic and symbolic value of this? Could Bunyan have given the geographical location of the City of Destruction?

5. How is the effect of bustle and hurry secured at the opening of this scene? Why is this effect desirable?

6. In what ways does Gloucester surprise you during the scene?

7. What additional evidence do you find in this scene that the play is better suited for reading than for the stage?

IV, 1.

1. What important element of Edgar's character is revealed in 1-9?

2. Why does not Edgar reveal his identity to his father during this scene?

3. How does the spiritual experience of Gloucester, as revealed here, parallel that of Lear? Give line references. How is it different from Lear's?

IV, 2.

1. What striking instance of dramatic irony do you find in this scene?

2. With 46-50 compare *Troilus and Cressida*, I, 3, 74-137, one of the greatest single speeches in Shakespeare and an amplification of Albany's thought. What is Albany's view of the whole situation?

3. When and how does Albany's prophecy reach fulfillment?

4. What adverse criticism have you to make upon Albany's conduct in this scene?

5. Comment upon 63b-67. Since Goneril has thrown off all the restraints of womanhood, is it anything more than sentimental folly to grant her those exemptions and prerogatives which should be granted only to true women?

6. Does Albany carry out the revenge mentioned in l. 97?

7. On the whole, does Albany seem the ideal man to restore order and " sustain the gored state " after the death of Lear?

IV, 3.

1. Why was it dramatically expedient that the King of France should not accompany Cordelia? May it be that Shakespeare consulted the patriotic feelings of his audience here?
2. Why did Cordelia smile at all, as reported in 18 *ff.*?
3. What is Kent's " dear cause," mentioned in l. 53?

IV, 4.

1. Why does the poet make Cordelia so explicit in justifying her invasion?

IV, 6.

1. Comment upon the stage effectiveness of 1–80.
2. Why is the pathos of this passage constantly in danger of passing into farce? By what means is it sustained and saved?
3. Cite passages of astonishing descriptive power. Note that Shakespeare, like Edgar, had learned to describe things vividly simply because the things themselves were not there. Why is *Merchant of Venice*, V, 1, 54–65, so excellent an example of this?
4. Comment closely upon the nature of Lear's thought in 83–191.
5. Find as many allusions to the lower animals as possible here and in the rest of the play. What is the value of this for the imagination? What line of thought led Lear, or rather, the poet, into it?
6. Explain the change in Gloucester made evident in 221 *ff.*
7. What dramatic purpose is served by Edgar's preservation of his disguise in 225 *ff.*?

IV, 7.

1. With l. 59b and following, compare III, 2, 19b–20.

What is the source or cause of the pathos?

2. Comment upon Cordelia's speeches made after her father awakes.

V, 1.

1. Explain 34–37.

V, 3.

1. Comment upon 16–17a with regard to Shakespeare's attitude toward the whole meaning and upshot of the play.

2. What is the source of the pathos in Lear's speeches, 8–25? It will probably be found that here, as often, pathos is due to a strong contrast between two ideas, one sub-conscious and the other expressed. The more the speaker neglects the former and stresses the latter, the more powerful is the resulting pathos. Greek tragedy affords many examples. Line 274 below is a supreme instance.

3. Enumerate all important contrasts between Lear's position and state of mind and heart in this scene and those in which he was presented in I, 1. Such contrasts, dealing in the more external and obvious way with the fails of princes, constituted for Shakespeare's audience the very essence and formula of tragedy. But it is most important to notice that the poet, while adhering to the formula and meeting his audience on its own ground, deepens, enriches, humanizes that formula almost beyond recognition.

4. With 30b–32a compare Napoleon Bonaparte's maxim: "The human heart is an enlarged vein which throbs more rapidly when one runs uphill."

5. Explain 73–74a. Compare ll. 96, 223–227, and V, 1, 34–37.

6. The critics who read their Shakespeare as a thesaurus of "wise saws and modern instances" have made much of 170–174, taking them as containing the "moral" which the poet wishes us to draw from the play. But note that this play is not a tragedy because people die

in it or because wickedness is punished, but because it states with godlike power and demoniac irony an enigma to which there is no answer. It tells us only that God sends his rain upon the just and the unjust alike. To miss this point is to miss all the deeper meaning of the drama and to miss the difference between art and homiletics. Compare this passage with IV, 1, 38–39a.

7. How is Edmund's delay in reprieving Lear and Cordelia made to seem natural? Note the absorbing interest of the events and the narrative intervening between his fight with Edgar and 242–246.

8. What tragic accident in *Romeo and Juliet* does this fatal delay of Edmund's recall? How does it heighten suspense? Note that the outcome, for the persons with whom we most deeply sympathize, might have been, but for this accident, supremely happy.

9. How has V, 2, led us to hope, for an instant, for a happy conclusion? By what other means has the poet given us "light at eventide," just before the final plunge into night?

10. How does this accident illustrate IV, 1, 38–39a? Do you think the poet planned the repentance of Edmund simply to make possible this final sardonic effect?

11. What is the irony in the close juxtaposition of l. 256a and the entrance of Lear?

12. In how many ways is Lear's majestic power, — physical, emotional, and intellectual, shown in 257–311? How and why does our sense of this power intensify our pity and heighten the effect of his death? Considering the king's great age, his exhausted condition, the trials he has just come through, the contrast with his great joy in V, 2, line 274, may well be regarded as the most intolerably pathetic line in the world's literature. Note that the captain's corroboration is added, so that we may not think Lear is boasting idly. But his killing of the hangman was the last flicker of the old fire. He falls immediately into childish babble.

13. How has Lear come to know so well that a voice soft, gentle, and low is "an excellent thing in woman"?

14. The moral mongers may agree that Lear deserved his fate, but what is to be said of Kent, the faithful, sinless, and self-forgetful, who sees all his noblest purposes brought to nought and who is barely recognized by the master for whom he dies ?

15. For how long after l. 276 does Lear apparently forget Cordelia ? To whom does " poor fool " refer in l. 305 ?

16. The beauty and daring of l. 309 have been frequently praised. Why ? But the preceding line is at least equally daring and equally inspired. Note the unerring instinct — or was it memory only ? — with which the poet cuts to the very heart of all bereavement.

17. Note the length of the words in 305–311a. From what language are they derived ? Latin ? French ? Old English ? Lear has called himself " every inch a king " and his command of noble speech has never belied him, but here he is, rather, every inch a man.

18. In the first scene of the play Lear takes a foolish pleasure in a false and simulated love. In the last scene, what? Lear's lesson is learned now. Where and how will he and Cordelia profit by that which has cost them both so much ? The sense of waste is always a large element in tragic effect. Note that Shakespeare does not appeal to a belief in an after life for an answer to these questions.

19. What appears to be the immediate cause of Lear's death ? Should 310–311a be spoken in sorrow or in an agony of joy ?

20. With 312b–315a compare 184b–186a and comment upon the characterization of Edgar and Kent, youth and age.

21. Note that in 317–320 Albany abdicates his legal rights. Why ? In all Shakespeare's tragedies some basis of future order is left. In *Hamlet*, Fortinbras. In *Macbeth*, Malcom. What here ? Has this basis been proved to be sufficient ?

22. With 321–322 compare 207–221 and 234b–236a. Inference ?

MACBETH

GENERAL QUESTIONS

1. Outline the action briefly. Why is it, on the whole, so simple and straightforward? Why so swift? Try to explain these features with reference to the character of the hero. Compare *Hamlet* in these regards.

2. Is the murder of Duncan the climax of the action? Why is it placed so early in the play?

*3. By what qualities does the hero command our admiration? To what degree and how long does he hold our sympathy also? Why is this necessary? Compare the sympathy and admiration elicited by Macbeth with that won and held by Romeo, Hamlet, Lear, Othello, Brutus, Coriolanus.

4. Should the play be considered any more a Tragedy of Macbeth than a Tragedy of Lady Macbeth. Why?

*5. Shakespeare's Tragic Muse gives no quarter to the incomplete, onesided man — the man who uses only part of his faculties. This is true of pitiless Nature also, and of the remorseless, passionate world of war and intrigue in which the poet's great heroes all live. Our modern world has erected barriers between the puny, the unfit, the "specialist" and that swift destruction which would have been his even five centuries ago. Shakespeare's heroes are never weaklings, but they are unfit, each at some one point, and specialists at other points. In Shakespeare's world, perfected and rounded strength is the strong man's only salvation. If character is the end of life, it was a better world than the safer, more comfortable world of to-day. Shakespeare's tragedies make their effects of "pity and terror" by showing that strength which is not rounded and complete becomes its own destruction. "Strengths by strengths do fail."

Fate strikes unerringly at the one crevice in the hero's armor. How does this apply in the case of each of the tragic heroes mentioned in question 3? Show that in each case the failure is tragic and arouses pity because it is allied to strength. When allied to weakness it is material for comedy, as in Molière.

6. Trace the gradual decay of Macbeth's moral nature. Is there any similar change in Lady Macbeth?

7. Discuss the part played by supernatural agencies in suggesting, inciting, and determining Macbeth's actions.

8. How and why does Lady Macbeth differ from her husband in her attitude toward the supernatural? What were the motives of her action?

9. Discuss the relative strength and nobility of Macbeth and his wife.

10. What characters in the play progress and develop, either for better or worse? What characters seem relatively static?

11. Compare Macbeth and his wife as to their relative fitness for plotting and for action. Contrast the two in other important respects.

12. What touches of "local color" do you find? Does the poet try to differentiate Scottish from English character? What part is played by landscape, climate, and weather in creating the general tone and atmosphere of the play? Do these differ importantly from what we should expect if the scene had been laid in England? What evidence do you find within the play that Shakespeare had visited Scotland?

13. Discuss the style of the play, especially as regards compression, vigor, directness, and virility.

14. Try to state the precise nature of the beauty of this play. It will be helpful to contrast it with *Antony and Cleopatra* or *Romeo and Juliet*. What tragedy or tragedies seem to you most like it in general effect? Answer such very general questions as this with all possible definiteness and precision.

DETAILED QUESTIONS

I, 1.

1. What is the meter employed here? Is it found elsewhere in the play? Compare *Midsummer Night's Dream*, II, 1, and *The Tempest*, V, 1, 88 *ff*. For what sort of effect does Shakespeare use this meter?
2. Defend the substitution of "and " for "or " in l. 2. How many questions are asked in the sentence as it stands? Is there anything in the character and powers of the witches that supports the reading " or "? Is there a hint that they intend to create or produce the weather in which they are to meet? Can you suggest any other clarifying emendation?
3. Comment upon the effect of the change of meter in l. 12.
4. Does this scene announce the key-note of the entire drama? What is the effect produced by it? Discuss the reasons for introducing the witches in the opening lines.

I, 2.

1. Is it made clear in this scene what the fighting is about? Is it necessary that we should know?
2. What does the scene accomplish in the way of exposition and characterization?

I, 3.

1. Is there any means of determining the length of time that elapses between the action of Scene 1 and that of the present scene?
2. What does the first witch propose to do to the Tiger? (*Ship*. With l. 9 compare 24–25.
3. With l. 38 compare I, 1, 11.
4. Answer the question put by Banquo in 51–52. Compare l. 139.
5. Why does Banquo see nothing to start at in the witches' prophecy?
6. With l. 46 compare *Merry Wives*, IV, 2, 202–205.

7. Carefully define the thought and feeling that actuate Macbeth in l. 86. Compare 118–120.

8. Estimate carefully the character and present mood of Macbeth as presented in this scene alone. Of Banquo.

9. What do Macbeth's associates think of him? Are they deceived?

10. What is your own theory as to the influence of the witches upon Macbeth? Is it a determining influence? Does it initiate a train of thought in his mind which leads to his later action?

11. How does the confirmation of a part of the witches' prophecy affect the mind of the hero? See l. 105 *ff.*

12. How does this scene advance the action?

13. Do you agree with the statement in 137–138? What trait of character is revealed here?

I, 4.

1. What is the dramatic irony in 11b–14a? Show that Shakespeare valued these lines more for their bearing on future events than for their application to the case of Cawdor. This is a good illustration of his exceedingly careful workmanship in this play.

2. How does the announcement in 35–39 affect Macbeth and, through him, the action of the entire play? See 48 *ff.*

3. What impression have you of the character of Duncan? The character seems to have been devised to meet the exigencies of the plot. How does it do so? With what character is Duncan's character in strong contrast?

I, 5.

1. When was this letter written, and when did Macbeth gain the knowledge referred to in 2–3? What is indicated by the fact that he has inquired about the witches? Where can he have applied for testimonials as to their powers?

2. Is the observation in l. 18 true to the facts of Macbeth's character as they have been represented? Is there a double characterization in this line?

3. Name three different kinds or phases of dramatic value in 16–31.

4. How do the soliloquies of Lady Macbeth differ from those of her husband?

5. State carefully the relations between husband and wife shown in 55–74.

I, 6.

1. What is the value of the descriptive passage, 1–10? Here, as so frequently in Elizabethan drama, description of landscape and the like have almost the value that stage carpentry and scene painting have for the modern drama. But there are other values here. What is indicated in these lines about the mood of the speakers? How does this mood contrast with that of Macbeth and his wife? Is there even a tinge of dramatic irony in the passage?

I, 7.

1. State precisely what considerations cause Macbeth to hesitate, judging from 1–12.

2. Is he troubled by moral scruples in 12–24?

3. Indicate three possible interpretations of "we fail," l. 59b. How do you think the actress should speak the two words?

II, 1.

1. With l. 3 compare II, 3, 24 *ff*. At what hour do Macduff and Lenox enter in Scene 3? What, then, is the time of night at which this and the following scene occur?

2. What is the mood of Banquo in 1–10? Does he suspect that evil is on foot? Is he morally blameless?

3. What are the motives behind the speeches in 11–30?

4. What action or "business" should intervene between the speaking of l. 32 and that of l. 33?

5. Should the phantom dagger be presented in any way to the eyes of the spectators in stage performance? Discuss fully.

6. What convinces Macbeth that the dagger is not real?

What special power of his mind is indicated in his ability
to criticize his own sensations ?

7. Enumerate the elements of horror and fear accumulated
   in the second half of Macbeth's soliloquy. How is l. 61
   highly characteristic of the speaker ?

8. What are the main divisions of this scene ?

II, 2.

1. What is the inference from 1–2 ? Just what is it that
   Lady Macbeth really fears in 10–11 ?

2. Comment upon 13b–14. Does this sentence show a trait
   of character which Macbeth does not share ? How is
   this trait shown later ?

*3. Would the presentation of the murder on the stage have
   added to or detracted from the terror of this scene ?
   Compare with Greek tragedy. French critics, with
   Greek models in mind, have considered English tragedy
   very bloody, and Shakespeare does not hesitate in other
   plays, or even in the present one, from presenting scenes
   of violence and horror. Do you consider the murder of
   Duncan what the French call a *scène à faire* — a piece
   of action that should be shown on the stage ?

4. What is the nature of Macbeth's fear in the remainder
   of the scene ? How and why has he changed since II, 1 ?
   Does he seem to be so much in command of himself
   and of the situation as he was earlier ? Relate this to
   his character as previously shown.

*5. Contrast Macbeth's emotional state with that of his
   wife. What is the secret of her comparative calm ?
   Who is responsible for the murder ? On this point, see,
   if possible, Corson's *Introduction to Shakespeare*,
   pp. 246–251.

6. With 51–52 compare I, 4, 52b–53. With 64–65 compare V, 1, 30–39. Explain.

*7. Study and comment upon De Quincey's essay *On the
   Knocking at the Gate in Macbeth*. It is to be found
   in the Furness *Variorum* and the *First Folio* edition
   and in De Quincey's *Works*. Compare *Othello*, V, 2,
   83 *ff.*

II, 3.

1. What two purposes are served by the scene of the drunken porter? Why is the scene written in prose? What is the effectiveness of his likening himself to the porter of hell gate?
2. Does Macbeth act his part well before Macduff and Lennox? Has there been another change in him?
3. Comment upon the murder of the grooms. Was it wisely done? Does it show that Macbeth has already outstripped his wife in crime? What further evidence is there of this?
4. Does Lady Macbeth fail, in a measure, in this scene? Is her fainting real or feigned?
5. What mistake is made by Malcolm and Donalbain?

II, 4.

*1. What is gained by the introduction of the Old Man? Compare *Richard II*, III, 4, the mob scenes in *Julius Cæsar* and *Coriolanus* and the common people in *Romeo and Juliet*.
*2. Comment upon the use of symbols in 11–20. See also II, 3, 57–66a. Compare with the use of symbols in Ibsen's later plays and in Maeterlinck. Is there any special significance in l. 18b?
3. State carefully the mood of Macduff. Are his suspicions aroused?

III, 1.

1. What three important purposes are served by Banquo's speech?
2. Do you see any special significance in l. 23?
3. With 55–57 compare *Antony and Cleopatra*, II, 3, 18–22. Does this indicate that the plays were written at about the same time?
*4. What is the etymology and history of the word "genius," l. 56?
5. Paraphrase 75b–84a, 116–118a, 128–133.
6. Does the style of these speeches seem in keeping with

the station in life of those addressed and with Macbeth's purpose ? Does Macbeth show himself an efficient and resourceful man in his treatment of the murderers ?

III, 2.

1. Can you answer the question asked in l. 8 *ff.* ?
2. What sort of emotion raises Macbeth to imaginative and poetic speech ?
3. What change has come about in the relations of husband and wife ? Give line references, citing comparisons from earlier scenes.

III, 3.

1. Support the view that Macbeth himself is the third murderer. Compare III, 4, 17–18.
2. Explain 11–14 by reference to the exigencies of Elizabethan staging.
3. For what reasons may this scene be considered the climax of the play ?

III, 4.

1. Explain l. 14. Is it grammatically correct ?
2. Paraphrase 33–37.
3. Comment upon any incongruities you find in the handling of the ghost's appearances. Note that the ghost is seen by the spectators as well as by Macbeth, but not by those about the table. Compare *Hamlet*, III, 4. How does this bear upon question 5 in II, 1 ?
4. Upon whom does the irony of l. 41 recoil ?
5. Make suggestions for the acting of 46–50.
*6. What is the etymology and history of the word " passion," l. 57 ?
7. Has Lady Macbeth lost her influence over her husband ? Explain.
8. What seems to be the immediate cause of the ghost's second entrance ? Is this true also of the first entrance ?
9. Is there any analogy between these appearances and the first appearance of the Weird Sisters ?

10. Consider the suggestion that one of the ghosts in this scene may be that of Duncan.

11. Does Macbeth tell the truth in 99–106 ? Could he face without flinching almost any terrors except those which he is called upon to face ?

12. Paraphrase 112b–113.

13. In what state of mind do you imagine the guests as leaving the palace ?

14. What important revelations of a change in Macbeth are given toward the end of the scene ? What radical change in his relations with his wife do you discover ?

III, 5.

1. After comparison of this scene with the earlier witch scenes, what reasons do you find for the common ascription of these lines to some writer — probably Middleton — other than Shakespeare?

2. Comment upon the verse of this scene.

3. Is there an inconsistency between 15–17 and the general spirit of the play?

4. What is the meaning of "security" in l. 32. Compare *Hamlet*, I, 5, 61.

5. How and why do the witches change in attitude toward Macbeth ? Does this indicate a corresponding change in his fortunes generally ?

6. Judging from 32–33, how do the witches intend to carry out their purposes ?

III, 6.

1. Compare this scene with II, 4. What is its purpose? Compare the manner of Macduff in II, 4, with that of Lennox in the present scene.

2. What dramatic purpose is served by Lennox's ironical recital of Macbeth's crimes?

IV, 1.

1. Do you think 39–43 were not written by Shakespeare? Why?

2. What later developments of the tragedy are fore-shadowed by the three apparitions?

3. How do the words spoken by the apparitions bear upon III, 5, 32–33 ?

4. Are there signs that 125–132 are an interpolation ? Note that, like 39–43, their chief purpose is to serve as introduction to a dance and music. Do these things, and more especially the song " Black Spirits," — which Shakespeare did not write, — harmonize perfectly with the tone of the play in general? Does it seem that some one has tried to make over the somber tragedy into something more like a masque ?

5. Learn from any annotated edition of the play the full meaning of l. 121. Show that this line was designed to appeal in a special manner to the poet's English audience. What bearing has this line upon the theory that the play was written to celebrate the accession of King James I of England, or at least with the intention of pleasing him?

6. What two original weaknesses of Macbeth's character are shown by 144–154 to have been increased by his recent experiences?

7. Has your admiration for Macbeth been sustained, in any measure, up to the present point? Does it end here?

8. Enumerate the forces now at work against Macbeth.

IV, 2.

1. What purpose is served by the dialogue between Lady Macduff and her son? In what ways does the dialogue fail to satisfy and please?

2. Do you think the violence of this scene should have been shown rather than merely reported? Is there any reason why it had to be shown? Compare the murder of Duncan.

3. How does the slaughter of Macduff's household differ from the previous crimes of Macbeth? What change in his character does it indicate ? What is its effect?

IV, 3.

1. Why does Malcolm distrust Macduff? Compare l. 25 and 117–118.
2. Why does Malcolm accuse himself of imaginary wickedness? Is he entirely insincere? Compare *Hamlet*, III, 1, 123–133.
3. How does Macduff receive the several self-accusations of Malcolm ?
4. How does the episode dealing with the " king's evil " — 140–159 — provide contrast with the state of affairs in Scotland? Is this a good way to flatter and compliment the new Scotch king of England? Is there any other reason for the introduction here of such apparently irrelevant material ?
5. What is the finest line spoken by Macduff after learning of his sorrow? Compare *Julius Cæsar*, IV, 3, 149 *ff.*
6. Do you think it was well done to postpone the careful delineation of Malcolm and Macduff until so late in the play? Has anything been gained by this?

V, 1.

1. How many scenes have passed since Lady Macbeth last appeared? What does this indicate?
2. What did Lady Macbeth probably write on the paper which she later sealed?
3. Explain " throw her nightgown upon her." Compare II, 2, 70.
4. With l. 39 *ff.* compare II, 2, 67.
5. Connect Lady Macbeth's words, from l. 47 on, with previous occurrences.
6. What do you find particularly effective in 56–58?

V, 2.

1. What is the purpose of this scene?
2. Why did Shakespeare feel free in this play to depict so favorably a revolt against a sovereign? In *Richard II* it had to be done more carefully.

V, 3.

1. Carefully describe Macbeth's mood in this scene.
2. What is the effect of the passages of philosophical reflection? Do they seem in character?
3. By what means does the poet soften the picture of Macbeth's moral and spiritual degradation?
4. What passages of pure and high poetry do you find in this scene?

V, 4.

1. Paraphrase 14b–16a.

V, 5.

1. To whom does Macbeth speak in 9–15a and 17–28? What are the possible meanings of "should" in l. 17? Which seems the most likely one?
2. Memorize 17–28.
3. How are Macbeth's moral degradation and his increasing reliance upon the supernatural emphasized in this scene?

V, 6 and 7.

1. What would be the effect of these scenes upon a stage such as that at the Globe Theater?

V, 8.

1. Does Shakespeare wish us to suppose that Macbeth was overcome because of the fact reported in 13b–16a or because of his knowledge of that fact and the influence of that knowledge upon him? How is this shown? What part is played by Macbeth's superstition in bringing about his death?
2. Show that the immediate causes of Macbeth's death are in close relation to important events of his life.
3. How are the closing events of the play knitted to the future? Compare the last scenes of *Hamlet* and *King Lear*.

CORIOLANUS

GENERAL QUESTIONS

1. Outline the plot. How many actions or stories do you find? Point out several instances of economy in incident and in *dramatis personæ*. For an example of the former, see V, 1. Do you find a case of the latter in Menenius and the tribunes?

2. State the function of each act in the development of the character of the hero and his fortunes.

3. State carefully your attitude toward the hero at the end of Act I, under the following heads: Is his character one of tragic grandeur? Have your sympathy for him and admiration of him been enlisted sufficiently to insure tragic "pity and terror" at sight of his fall? If so, by what means? Wherein has the poet come dangerously near to forfeiting this sympathy for his hero?

*4. What dangers foreshadowing a tragic conclusion are clearly indicated in Act I? Are these dangers chiefly within or chiefly without the mind and character of the hero? Is this latter feature characteristic of modern as opposed to ancient tragedy? Why?

5. Show, if possible, that the ruin of Coriolanus is brought on by a fault that is inherent in his nobility — a " defect of his qualities." Show that he is tried and that he fails at just the one point in which he is weak. How much of our pity and sense of tragic waste is due to the fact that his weakness is made to seem almost a necessary part of the unquestionable nobility for which we honor him?

6. What fundamental motive for Coriolanus's ardent service of his country is revealed in the last two acts? Is this the highest possible motive?

7. Comment upon IV, 7, 35–55, item by item, as a treat-

ment in full of the character and fortunes of the hero
and therefore of the theme of the play. Does this passage
seem to express the poet's own attitude and judgment?

8. Who is the most powerful person in the play — the one
who really controls destiny and shapes his own life?
Can this be said of the hero? In what sense is Coriolanus a hero? Romain Rolland has said: "No man is
strong from reason, but from passion." Do you know
of any exception to this among Shakespeare's heroes?
Does Coriolanus's weakness as well as his strength proceed from passion rather than reason?

9. In what respects does this great play seem the product
of a mood of somber, misanthropic pessimism?

10. Do you find evidence that Shakespeare takes sides between the aristocrats and the plebs? What is the testimony of this play in regard to the question of the
poet's anti-democratic sympathies? Compare the play,
in this aspect of it, with *Julius Cæsar*. Does the play
deal in an argumentative and propagandist spirit with
political theories, or is it primarily a study of egoism?

11. Try to express in a few words the total effect of the
play upon you. In what respects does it take very high
rank among the poet's achievements? Why must it be
ranked, after all, somewhat lower than his greatest
tragedies? What other play or plays does it most resemble in structure? In theme? In total effect?

12. If this play were now first discovered, by what means
would you try to establish the date of its composition
and its position among the poet's works? Could you
show that it must be a late play but yet not the latest?
How? Does it betray any signs of declining power?

DETAILED QUESTIONS

I, 1.

1. What is the dramatic purpose of 1–50?

2. Is Menenius successful in 56–167? Does he **deserve**
success?

3. What can be said in favor of the citizens in this scene? What against them? It should be remembered throughout the play that Shakespeare lived long before the age of Liberalism and of Socialism, that he is not discussing social theories but is writing a tragedy dealing with the ruin of a great individual, and finally, that his treatment of the mob, here and everywhere, was largely dictated by the necessity of providing a suitable background for the hero.

*4. Do you think Tolstoy's ideal of a drama in which the masses take the place of the hero — the highly-gifted, highly-privileged individual — is capable of realization? See Tolstoy's *What Is Art?* Does it seem that tragedy is committed by its very nature to the "great man" theory of society and history? What modern writers have attempted a drama in which *demos* takes the place of the supreme individual? Have they succeeded? Diderot is a good example and initiates the movement. Remembering that Shakespeare's choice of kings and men in high position for his heroes, while it is not accidental, is not essential to his theory, state whether you consider Ibsen and his followers good exponents of the democratic theory of drama.

5. Is it clear from the present scene that Shakespeare himself scorns the common people, or do we gain this impression only from the polite contempt of Menenius and the scathing denunciations of Coriolanus?

*6. Summarize the main points made in Coriolanus's diatribe, 171–192. How much of this proves true later? Find similar passages in *Richard II* and *Julius Cæsar*.

7. What mistakes do the tribunes make in their estimate of Coriolanus? Why?

8. What exposition in this scene? What notes of danger are clearly struck? How is suspense secured? Give reasons for considering this an excellent first scene.

I, 2.

1. What is the purpose of this scene? What part of scene 1 does it continue?

I, 3.

1. What character contrasts are presented here? Do they seem natural and convincing or somewhat forced? Point out all the minor touches by which they are accentuated.
2. Would you choose Volumnia or Virgilia for a mother? Which for a wife? Did Fate choose well for Coriolanus?
3. Is Volumnia intended as a typical Roman mother? Note especially 20–27. Is her type less familiar to-day than in earlier ages? What substitute for military glory is allowed to-day by mothers of this type?
4. Point out all the ways in which the characterization of Coriolanus is advanced in this scene, in which he does not appear.
5. Virgilia is drawn with assured power and clear insight. Note her voluntary and useless martyrdom in remaining at home until her lord's return. She is firm — obstinate, rather — only in meaningless self-sacrifice. Why did Shakespeare provide the hero with such a wife? Is she " a helpmeet for him " ?
6. What is the effect upon the tone of the entire play of this peaceful domestic scene, this quiet-toned *genre* picture? Note the subjects of conversation.
*7. What possible symbolism in 62–71 ? Does Shakespeare make extensive use of hereditary traits in characterization ? Why is this ? Compare Ibsen, Schnitzler, Sudermann, or von Hoffmannsthal.

I, 4 to 8.

1. What sort of stage effect was intended in these scenes? Why are they so short and the entrances and exits so frequent ?
2. How does the poet attempt to conceal or atone for the poverty of his stage ? What double purpose is served by the single combat in Scene 8 ?

I, 9.

1. Explain Coriolanus's refusal of the booty and his dislike of extravagant praise. With the former, compare I,

5, 5–9. Is the latter perfectly sincere ? If we are right in considering Coriolanus a supreme egoist, is it not difficult to explain his shrinking from eulogy ? Is he modest here ?

2. What is the dramatic effect of the praise of Coriolanus by generals and soldiery ? Where is there a similar device used in *Othello* ?

3. Comment upon the famous words, "By Jupiter, forgot." Show that they heighten the illusion of reality. Does Coriolanus elsewhere show a poor memory? Is this in keeping with the headlong impetuosity of his life ? Note that he sincerely wishes to repay the poor Volscian but yet has forgotten his name. Is he thinking of his benefactor, primarily, or of himself ? Is it clear that even the kindliness of Coriolanus is marred and tainted by what George Meredith calls " that old devil of the thousand lures," the passion of Self ?

I, 10.

1. Why is Aufidius made to plot treachery against his rival ? Does this not unduly degrade the hero's enemy ? Does it serve to exalt Coriolanus in your eyes and add suspense ?

2. What has been the poet's chief effort in his treatment of the hero in this act ? If you knew nothing of Coriolanus but what is given in Act I, what would you say of him ? Why has the poet given as our first important impression a picture of Coriolanus in battle?

3. Besides the main theme of the act, there are several secondary themes that have a different bearing upon the hero's nature. What are they ?

4. Are all the essential components of the play's action found, at least in the germ, in this act ?

II, 1.

1. Summarize briefly the opinion Menenius gives of himself in 51–72. Is he sincere in these lines ? Are such men as Menenius especially given to confessions of this sort, — making virtues out of faults ?

2. Show the contrast, item for item, between the opinion Menenius gives of himself and that which he gives of the tribunes in 74–106.

3. Is Menenius here defending Coriolanus, himself, or the aristocratic point of view in government and society?

4. Does Menenius voice the poet's own view of the tribunes and their activities?

5. What is the purpose of 107–220? Is any new light thrown upon any of the characters?

6. Comment closely upon the exquisitely managed part of Virgilia.

7. Show that there is double-edged characterization in l. 192a.

8. What dramatic value have 240–247a? What motive actuates the tribunes in their enmity towards the hero?

9. Into what divisions does this scene fall? State the purpose of each.

II, 2.

1. Do you think the officers are better fitted than any previous speakers to give an unprejudiced view of the situation? Do you think their speeches may be accepted as a sort of chorus, stating the truth as the poet wishes us to see it?

2. What is the motive of the speaker in 74b–75a and later in the scene?

3. What elements of suspense in this scene?

4. Why is Cominius's praise of the hero given just here?

II, 3.

1. What is the purpose and effect of 1–43? Where did the plan of action mentioned in 44–52 originate and what is its purpose?

2. Explain the use of rhyme in 120–131. Paraphrase 124b–128a.

3. How do the events of this scene illustrate I, 1, 171 *ff.*?

4. In how much do you sympathize with the hero in this scene?

5. How does the second act contrast with the first in the picture it gives of the hero? Explain differences.

III, 1.

1. Show that the hero is attacked on his weakest side in 1–180.
2. What dramatic irony in 107b–112a?
3. Discuss l. 255. Does it tell the truth?
4. What excites Coriolanus's outbreak in the earlier part of the scene? Compare III, 3, 25–30. Show that this cause continues in operation. What other tragic heroes of Shakespeare show the same weakness?
5. Paraphrase 140–161.
6. Outline carefully the thought of 140–161. How much truth and wisdom do you find in these weighty lines? Compare the great speech on "degree" in *Troilus and Cressida*, I, 3, 75–137. Does it seem probable that Shakespeare is expressing his own convictions in these speeches, considering the power and vigor with which they are written?
7. What has been the tribunes' plan of action? Has it been well executed? Was it based upon a sufficiently clear knowledge of the hero's character?
8. Comment upon the rabble scenes here and later with regard not to their literary but to their theatrical merits.
9. Account for the intensity and absorbing interest of this scene.

III, 2.

1. How do 7–13 soften our judgment against the hero?
2. Characterize briefly the counsel of Volumnia. What is the exact difference between her and her son? Which seems nearer right? Which shows greater knowledge of the world?
3. Is the nobler or the baser Coriolanus in the ascendant in this scene? Note the immense power of his speeches near the end, indicating the rage which he struggles to master. What sort of man, according to the Bible, is "greater than he who taketh a city"?

4. Do we expect, at the end of this scene, that Coriolanus will be successful in his attempt to hoodwink the people? Why? Is this expectation of ours to his credit or not?

5. What suspense is created by the scene?

III, 3.

1. Are the new accusations here prepared true or false? After 1–30, what chance does the hero appear to have? Does this passage destroy suspense or does it create a new interest, namely, an interest in the strong man's method of action now that he is securely taken in the toils?

2. Where is the climax of the play — the point at which the forces for and against the hero waver for a moment and then those against suddenly gain the ascendant?

3. Do you blame Coriolanus for his actions in this scene, or is it clear that he is now simply reaping the penalty of former mistakes, his control over fortune having at last slipped away from him?

4. Do the tribunes answer 42–43a? Why?

5. With what earlier warning speech by Coriolanus should the titanic grandeur of 120–135 be compared? Is it conceivable that the poet could write these lines without profound sympathy for the point of view they present?

6. Judging from the present scene alone, would you say that Coriolanus's quarrel with the people has been actuated by patriotism or by baser motives?

7. What feeling is left at the end of this scene as to the future of Rome?

8. Why has the story of the fall of Coriolanus been protracted through three scenes?

IV, 1.

1. Paraphrase 1–11.

2. Point out all passages indicating that a plan of action is already nascent in Coriolanus's mind.

3. Define carefully the mood in which the hero accepts his defeat. Does he retain our sympathy in this scene?

IV, 2.

1. What is the effect of this scene upon your sympathy for Coriolanus and his group?

IV, 3.

1. What is the purpose of this scene? Does it seem necessary? Into what other scene might its essential material have been compressed?

IV, 4.

1. Why does the poet reveal the hero's treachery before the action of Scene 5?

IV, 5.

1. Show that Aufidius makes a better impression than the hero in nobility and generosity of feeling. Is this morally and æsthetically right? What is its dramatic purpose? The moral and dramatic aspects of this beautifully constructed play are inseparably united. This statement cannot be made of all of Shakespeare's greatest plays.
2. Why do you think the poet framed this scene between the two appearances of the serving-men? Is the scene within adequately reported by the third serving-man? Note that this arrangement saves a stage setting for the banquet room and that it requires fewer actors. But there are other reasons.
3. How does the action of the serving-men resemble that of the plebeians in other parts of the play and confirm Coriolanus's opinion of the common people?

IV, 6.

1. Outline the gradual but swift development of the war tidings up to the point at which their full weight and import are felt by all classes.
2. Define carefully the mood and thought of Menenius in this scene. Note and explain his repetition of words and phrases in 87 *ff*.

3. Comment upon the part played by the citizens. Show that they only repeat former actions and confirm the truth of I, 1, 171 *ff.*

4. What dramatic irony do you find in this scene?

IV, 7.

1. Coleridge calls the passage 28–57 "the least explicable from the mood and full intention of the speaker of any in Shakespeare." He means, apparently, that he cannot reconcile Aufidius's envy of Coriolanus with his praise of him. Can you? Note that even the lieutenant is forced to praise even while he fears the hero. "For when our foes do praise, such fame speaks clear." How much more, then, the far nobler Aufidius! Has there been sufficient characterization of Aufidius to warrant us in calling his action here inconsistent? Compare the last speech of the play.

2. Do you feel that Aufidius or Shakespeare is speaking in 35–55 ? Which of the three interpretations of Coriolanus's character seems most satisfactory? Has each of them some element of truth?

3. This passage, in its amazing mastery of all resources of verbal expression, is worthy of a place beside the speeches of Æneas in *Troilus and Cressida* or the soliloquies of Hamlet. Paraphrase it carefully in the fewest possible words but rendering every shade of thought of the original. How does your number of words compare with that of Shakespeare?

4. What two main purposes did the poet have in this scene?

V, 1.

1. Outline the thought and motives of Menenius in 1–62.

2. How are 47b–58 in harmony with the speaker's character? Do we expect him to succeed?

V, 2.

1. Note resemblances between the situation and action presented here and those of *II Henry IV*, V, 5. Account for differences.

2. Since the action of this and the preceding scene leads to nothing, why was it presented? What is its effect upon our estimate of the action of Scene 3?

3. Coriolanus took no force of men with him when he left Rome. He leads only one half of Aufidius's army, the whole of which has been beaten by Rome. What is the effect, then, of Rome's consternation and its successive appeals to him? Why would such a situation be impossible in modern warfare? Why was it possible under the conditions of mediæval warfare which, of course, Shakespeare had primarily in mind?

V, 3.

1. Outline Volumnia's appeal. What conquers Coriolanus?

2. Does Coriolanus's decision do him credit or is his present action morally neutral, necessitated by faults and actions lying farther back?

3. Considering the suspense, emotional intensity, and interplay of character in this scene, do you regard it as on the whole the most brilliant and memorable scene in the play? Is its preëminence due to the admirable situation which was given to the poet by history or legend, or is it due to his masterly handling of that situation?

V, 4 and 5.

1. What is the dramatic purpose of these scenes and what is their bearing upon the events of the last scene?

2. In what earlier passage have we observed something like this gradual transpiring of important news? What psychological or æsthetic explanation of the device can you offer?

V, 6.

1. With 85–90 compare III, 1, 86–90, and III, 3, 65–73, and comment. Show how Aufidius's plan resembles throughout and in detail the plan with which the tribunes were successful. Is this done in order to show that the hero has not changed, has not learned from

his first lesson, and that, indeed, he cannot or will not be taught, in this life?

2. How do the charges made by Aufidius in 91–101 affect your sympathies? Why is this necessary at this point?

3. Is the death of the hero brought about by the natural outworking of character or by chance? Is this essential to tragic effect?

ANTONY AND CLEOPATRA

GENERAL QUESTIONS

1. Learn the main facts regarding the lives of Octavius Cæsar, Lepidus, Antony, Sextus Pompeius, Enobarbus, Mæcenas, Cleopatra, Octavia. See Furness's *Variorum Edition*, pp. 1–9.

2. Criticize the structure of the play, especially of Acts II, III, and IV. Explain this by referring to the nature of the poet's material and compare similar effects in his chronicle plays.

3. Discuss Boas's remark : "The multiplicity of details is bewildering and no single event stands out boldly as the pivot on which the catastrophe turns." Do you discover here the common critical error of assuming that one knows beforehand the effect which the artist desired or should have desired to produce ?

4. What effect has this same "bewildering multiplicity" in producing the play's surpassing interest, its amazing richness and variety ? Are we left in any doubt as to what series of events produces the catastrophe ?

5. Why would it have been a grave artistic error to have made the action and structure of this play simple, clear, obvious, like that, say, of *Julius Cæsar?* Shakespeare attended no school for dramatists except that which he found on the public stage. He did not run all of his dramatic material into one common mould as the academic critics of his own and of later times would have had him do, but each new story took the dramatic form and structure which suited it best. The present play has the wavering fluidity of life and it is for this reason, chiefly, that age cannot wither it or custom stale its infinite variety.

*6. Does the play preserve any one of the three Aristotelian
"unities"? Compare its structure with that of Dryden's splendidly beautiful reworking of the same material along "classical" lines — *All for Love*. What
does Dryden gain by excision, compression, and reshap-
ing? What does he lose?

7. Trace carefully the series of events leading to Antony's
death. What is the immediate cause of his suicide?
What elements of the play justify the name "tragedy"?

8. In Acts III and IV note evidences of Cleopatra's
power over Antony making for his ruin and downfall.
Is she anywhere clearly untrue to him? Is she anywhere a help and strength to him?

9. What, exactly, was the nature of the love of Antony
and Cleopatra, judging from their age, their characters, and all other indications? Compare the love of
Romeo and Juliet.

10. Write a careful study of Cleopatra, based upon de-
monstrable facts, not fancies or vague generalities, and
relying upon citations from the text for support.

11. Select ten passages that seem to you to have extraordinary poetic splendor and beauty. Memorize at least
twenty-five lines.

12. State in a few words the effect of this play upon you.
If you were never to read it again, what feature of it
would shine longest in your memory? In what respects
does it stand among the greatest things of Shakespeare's creation? In what ways is it inferior to his
best mature work?

DETAILED QUESTIONS

I, 1.

1. How is the action of the play linked to past time in
this scene?

2. What is the purpose of Cleopatra in 19–24a?

3. Do you consider the stage direction for l. 37, first made
by Pope, appropriate to the situation?

4. Paraphrase 41–42.
5. What are the relations existing between Antony and Cleopatra, according to the indications of this scene? Does it indicate fairly well the relations which they continue to hold toward each other throughout the play?
6. What exposition in this scene?

I, 2

1. The play opens in the year 40 B.C. Charmian is about eighteen years old. Compare the *Gospel, according to Saint Matthew*, II, 8, and comment upon the possible reference in 25–30. What sort of effect was the poet trying for in this obscure reference? Why did he make it so obscure?
2. Compare l. 89 with l. 91 and comment upon Cleopatra's method of treating Antony. What may be her object in this?
3. Comment upon the manner in which Antony receives the news from Rome. What is indicated regarding his character and present frame of mind?
4. Comment upon l. 150.
5. Why does Antony take just this time, l. 162, to announce the death of Fulvia? Compare l. 183.
6. What is the attitude of Enobarbus in these speeches? What is he trying to do?
7. Into what divisions does this scene fall? What is the function of each?

I, 3.

1. Do you agree with Charmian or with Cleopatra in 1–12?
2. How should the words "married woman," l. 20, be spoken by the actress? What is the whole weight of meaning that Cleopatra gives to them?
3. Has there been an earlier statement of the idea in 27–29? Does Cleopatra speak sincerely here?
4. What is the etymology of "scrupulous," l. 48? What is its meaning here?
5. Which wins in the encounter of this scene? Why?

I, 4.

1. Paraphrase and explain 49b–50.
2. In what sense is Antony hero of this play? Compare the heroic qualities of Romeo or of Othello. What character endangers this position of Antony in the spectator's sympathy? Is the danger avoided in the present scene? How?
3. What is the dramatic effect of 55b–71a? Comment upon the character of Cæsar as shown in this speech and scene.
4. What exposition in this scene?

I, 5.

1. Trace carefully the emotional changes mirrored by the words of 19–34.
2. Is Cleopatra sincere in 66–75?
3. What is the purpose and function of this scene?

II, 1.

1. What is the character of Pompey as shown here?
2. Are Menas and Menecrates distinguished carefully from each other?
3. What information is given in this scene?
4. Consider Johnson's suggestion that this scene might have been Scene 6 of Act I.

II, 2.

1. In what different ways does Shakespeare use the word "stomach"? Compare l. 9.
2. Compare Lepidus's attitude in 1–14 with the statement made in II, 1, 14–16. What is his character?
3. What action accompanies l. 27a? Compare I, 1, 37. Remember that most of the "business" in Shakespeare rests upon the surmises of editors and upon a misty tradition.
4. Paraphrase and explain 45–54.
5. Characterize the conference between Cæsar and Antony.

6. Which of the two is in the right? Which makes the better use of the points in his favor? Which makes the better impression?

7. Do you think Dryden did well in *All for Love* in giving the substance of Enobarbus's description of Cleopatra to Antony? Was Hartley Coleridge right in thinking Enobarbus not a sufficiently "interesting person" to speak these glowing lines?

8. We are supposed to have Cleopatra moving and speaking before us. Then what advantage is gained by this long description of her person and character?

9. What are the divisions of this scene? What is the purpose of the second division?

II, 3.

1. What phase of Antony's character is illustrated in 5-7? Is the metaphor employed in these lines suited to the social position of the speaker?

2. What is the significance of the entrance of the soothsayer at just this point? How does the soothsayer happen to be here?

3. Is it the grammar or the sense which is at fault in 11-12a? What is the meaning of "motion" in l. 14?

4. With 17-23 compare *Macbeth* III, 1, 56-57.

5. Compare 39-40 with 5-7. What has caused the change? Should this cause have been sufficient?

II, 4.

1. Purpose of this scene?

II, 5.

1. Many critics consider the reference to billiards in l. 3 a glaring anachronism. Supposing it is an anachronism, is it at all serious? There is good reason for thinking that the game was known in Greece in 400 B.C.

2. What phase of the speaker's character is shown in 10-15?

3. Why does Cleopatra repeatedly interrupt the messenger, continually surmising the worst?

4. Is her treatment of the messenger tragic or comic material? What effect has it here? Why?

II, 6.

1. Is this scene interesting in and for itself? How would the material it contains be handled by a modern dramatist?

II, 7.

1. This is a scene which the older type of criticism, based upon Aristotle, would have condemned as lacking in "decorum." According to this idea, a king should always act in a royal way on the stage and a soldier like a soldier, a beggar like a beggar. Shakespeare had probably heard of this canon of the schools, but he disregards it whenever it suits his purpose to do so. Richard II acts like a child, Falstaff like a coward, and Autolycus like a Bohemian poet. Do you find anything essentially inartistic in the presentation of the great Romans of this scene under the influence of drink?

2. How has wine affected the manner of each of those present? How is the character of each brought out?

3. What is accomplished by the scene?

III, 1.

1. What is the function of this scene?

III, 2.

1. What is the fitness of Agrippa's reference to the "Arabian bird"?

2. In what mood are 6–20 spoken?

3. Does it seem natural that Agrippa and Enobarbus should speak thus of Lepidus?

4. With 28–33 compare II, 6, 128–130.

5. Explain 47–50.

6. What does Octavia tell Cæsar? Compare 59b–61a.

7. Comment upon the character and mood of Enobarbus as shown in 50–59.

8. In the *Folios*, l. 59 reads "Believe't till I weepe too." Does this reading give better sense than the reading

"wept," first suggested by Theobald ? Argue in favor
of one or the other.

9. What action accompanies 61–64 ?
10. What lines from this scene do you consider most
beautiful, without reference to the context ?

III, 3.

1. With 16–17 compare *King Lear*, V, 3, 272–273.
Comment.
2. Do you notice in Charmian's speeches any change
from her former attitude toward Cleopatra ? Can you
account for it ?
3. What change has there been in the messenger since his
last appearance ?
4. Should Cleopatra have been shrewd enough to account
for this change and to allow for it ? Why is she not ?
What obscures her mind ?
5. Is there any evidence that Shakespeare was thinking
of Queen Elizabeth in his treatment of Cleopatra in
this scene ?
6. What is the dramatic effect of Charmian's speeches toward the close of the scene ?

III, 4.

1. What is Antony's purpose here ? To soothe and quiet
Octavia or to prepare for desertion of her ? Support
either opinion by line references.

III, 5.

1. Why are the first lines in prose ? Account for the
change to verse.
2. What is the advantage of presenting the material of
this scene in narration rather than in action ?
3. What "moral lesson" may be drawn from the fate of
Lepidus ?

III, 6.

1. Does Cæsar seem just and reasonable, according to his
own account, in 24–37 ?

2. Do you agree with Corson's opinion that the extravagance of Cæsar's language in 43 *ff.* is due to insincerity? To what other causes might it be due?

3. What element in Cæsar's character makes it possible for him to claim so much honor as his sister's due and at the same time to treat her so hardly?

4. Note and comment upon Octavia's indifference, 76b–78a, to the list of royal names Cæsar speaks with such evident pleasure.

5. In what ways are 81–85 a fitting speech of such a man as Cæsar to a woman?

6. What is the effect of 86a and 89b–90a?

7. By what means is Octavia finally silenced and her whole mission brought to nought?

8. Basing your judgment upon this scene alone, state the most important ways in which Octavia contrasts with Cleopatra.

9. By what means could a woman win any large measure of freedom and power in the ancient world? Does Shakespeare show Cleopatra employing these means? Does Octavia fail because she cannot or will not employ them?

III, 7.

1. What is indicated by Enobarbus's repetitions in his first speeches?

2. Contrast the claims made by Cleopatra with those made by Octavia in the preceding scene? Which is nearer right, according to modern standards? What did Shakespeare think about this?

3. Why is Antony determined to fight at sea?

4. Point out two speeches in this scene in which Antony's folly is probed to the quick. Show by reference to other parts of the play that the person who speaks them may be regarded as a "chorus character," or one who speaks, to a certain degree, the mind of the dramatist.

III, 8 and 9.

1. Compare the military manner of Cæsar with that of Antony in the previous scene.

2. For what theatrical effect did the poet design these short scenes? What peculiarity of his stage made them possible? How were they acted on his stage? How acted on the modern stage?

III, 10.

1. What advantage is gained by the narrative method employed here?
2. Study *The Tempest*, I, 1, and suggest another and possibly more telling way of presenting the material of the scene.
3. What difficulty do you find in understanding and interpreting the flight of Antony? Is this difficulty due to the use of the narrative method?

III, 11.

1. Judging from Antony's horror at his deed, does it not seem that he must have undergone a considerable struggle at the time it was committed? Does this reveal another fault in the method employed in Scene 10?
2. What action do you imagine as accompanying 25–35?
3. How does Antony apologize before Cleopatra for his act? Is he sincere?
4. Does Antony's closing speech, 69 *ff.*, seem entirely noble?

III, 12.

1. What is Cæsar's opinion of women, as shown here? Has it been fully indicated before? Is it significant? In what other plays has Shakespeare characterized men by showing their attitudes towards women?

III, 13.

1. Do you wholly agree with 3–12? What is Enobarbus's purpose in these lines? What is the dramatic purpose of the lines? Can you explain 29–37a in the same way?
2. Paraphrase 31b–34a. Comment fully upon l. 46a. Does it in any way affect the illusion of reality? What is the speaker's place in the story? He is one of the most baffling characters in Shakespeare.

3. Is Enobarbus's change of sides well handled? Do you fully understand his motives? Are the character and motives of Enobarbus clear at any time?

4. Is Antony's treatment of the servitors so exceptional as Enobarbus and Cleopatra seem to think it? What other examples do you find of his friendly treatment of inferiors?

5. Comment closely upon the character of Cleopatra as shown in 46–85.

6. Is 195–201 a statement of the poet's judgment upon Antony which he wishes us to adopt?

7. Is there something especially ugly and displeasing in the portraiture of Antony and Cleopatra in this scene?

8. What outcome of Antony's fortunes do we now expect? How have we been led to expect this?

IV, 2.

1. Carefully describe Antony's mood.

IV, 4.

1. What is there especially beautiful and pleasing in this scene? By what means does the poet contrive to restore our sympathy to Antony and Cleopatra? Why does he do so at just this point?

IV, 5.

1. Is Enobarbus's action here in harmony with his character as previously shown? Comment upon Antony's acceptance of the news.

IV, 7 and 8.

1. What dramatic effect is made by representing Antony as victorious on the first day?

IV, 9.

1. Has Enobarbus been presented as a man of emotional intensity sufficient to make it possible for him to die of heartbreak?

2. Does the knowledge of his death and of its cause influence your opinion of Antony in any way?

IV, 14.

1. What elements of this scene combine to make it of particularly intense and thrilling interest?
2. By what means does Antony, here and earlier, win our love even though our respect for him may be nearly or quite gone?

IV, 15.

*1. Describe the Elizabethan stage setting of this scene.
2. What is the source of the pathos in 18–21a? Note especially the wonderful rhythm and cadence of the speech — a cadence and rhythm in which the normal beat of the blank verse line plays but a minor part. This passage affords an admirable example of Shakespeare's later style at its best. The rhythm of thought and emotion dominates whole sentences, constantly threatening to overwhelm the steady beat of the decasyllables but never quite doing so. Memorize these lines.
3. Comment upon the merits of this scene as a stage spectacle or tableau.
4. Select two or three passages, aside from the supreme one noted above, in which the expression seems as near perfection as words can be made to go — the verse throbbing in every syllable beneath the weight of passion which it has to bear.
5. What other elements not yet mentioned contribute to make this scene one of the most powerfully affecting in Shakespeare?
6. What change in Cleopatra is caused by and partially revealed in the events of the scene?
7. With the word "sport" in l. 32 compare II, 5, 10–15. There is a piercing irony here which the poet's audience must have missed and which the reader may easily overlook.

V, 1.

1. What dramatic purpose is served by showing Cæsar's sorrow at the death of Antony?

V, 2.

1. What is the effect intended in Cleopatra's praise of Antony?

2. What is the effect of the episode of Seleucus?

3. How does 215b–221a increase the "illusion of the stage"? How would l. 220 especially have this effect upon Shakespeare's stage?

4. Can you justify on æsthetic grounds the introduction of comic material at this point? Compare the Grave-digger Scene in *Hamlet* and the Drunken Porter in *Macbeth*.

5. What is the secret of the strange, compelling power of 311c–313a? What double contrast do the lines suggest?

6. Follow closely the parts of Charmian and Iras. Why and how does Iras die? When did Charmian first poison herself? Complete Charmian's sentence broken off at l. 322.

7. Do you accept the opinion of Bernard Shaw that the unquestionable sublimity of this scene is a "theatrical sublimity" and that its pathos is a "stage pathos"? Even if we find these statements largely true, we need not despair. The Shavian type of mind was not widely represented in Shakespeare's audiences. Even to-day, the man who can smile disdainfully at this mimic sorrow is not to be envied.

THE TEMPEST

GENERAL QUESTIONS

1. Enumerate the actions of the play. Which is the main action? What important contrasts do you find between the actions? Point out the more important character contrasts.

2. Point out and comment upon the large amount of spectacle in the play. Note also the many references to music and the frequent songs. Show that the play is vaguely similar to the masque, a form of drama in great vogue when *The Tempest* was written.

3. This play was produced at court during the festivities celebrating the marriage of Princess Elizabeth, 1613. Elizabeth was then fifteen years of age. From I, 2, 40–41, 53–54, estimate the age of Miranda. What is the possible inference?

4. Do you think that the figure of Prospero may have been drawn as a portrait, very flattering indeed, of King James? How does this possibility recall *A Midsummer Night's Dream*? In what other respects are the two plays comparable?

5. In what sense or senses is this play "romantic"? In what ways is it "classical"?

*6. How much time elapses during the action? How many places are represented? Compare *Henry V* or *Antony and Cleopatra* in these two respects. To what part of a Greek drama does the narrative of Prospero in I, 2, correspond?

7. Select several passages showing Shakespeare's "overloaded style." Select other passages in which the thought itself, apart from its expression, is unusually profound and difficult to follow. Do you find it hard to follow the thread of the story? Does the poet seem forgetful of his audience in any parts or aspects of the drama? Are there any parts or aspects of the play in which he seems to be writing for himself as audience, as a lyric poet may?

8. Cite all passages bearing upon the view that Shakespeare was thinking of himself in drawing the character and situation of Prospero. Form your own opinion in regard to this matter.

9. Cite all passages bearing upon the view that in this play Shakespeare bade farewell to his art, in an allegorical fashion. Note especially Prospero's treatment of Ariel. What would be the function or significance of Ariel in such an allegory? Of Caliban? Of Miranda and Ferdinand? Was Shakespeare much given to the autobiographical or to the allegorical method — at least in his plays? Is there anything peculiar in the circumstances under which this play was written that may have offered special temptation?

10. Discuss the function of the supernatural in the play. In how far does it determine human action and in how far does it merely objectify the workings of the mind and conscience? Compare its function in *Macbeth*.

11. To what extent does Shakespeare embody in this play his final philosophy of life? Outline this philosophy, as you deduce it from the play, as clearly and simply as possible. Is this the best way to study Shakespeare — taking him as a moralist, a "man with a message"? Does he seem to have thought of himself as a preacher? Was he primarily concerned with an effort to answer the great unanswerable questions or with an attempt to ask them in the most telling and impressive way?

DETAILED QUESTIONS

I, 1.

1. Collect from this entire scene nautical terms not likely to be familiar to a landsman. Where did Shakespeare probably learn them?

2. Describe as accurately as you can the situation of the vessel and the measures taken.

3. How would this scene have been staged in Shakespeare's theater?

4. Are you made to sympathize with the mariners or with the courtiers? Is this usual in Shakespeare? Why is it done here?

5. What is the emotional effect of the scene? How may it have been enhanced in acting? How might the effect of 64–66 have been increased?

I, 2.

1. Comment fully upon the effect of 1–2 and of "some noble creature," l. 7.

2. What is the effect upon the audience of Prospero's repeated appeals to Miranda for attention? Does Shakespeare do this because he knows he is not managing his exposition as skillfully as usual?

3. Arrange 26–32 in intelligible prose, preserving the wording as far as possible.

4. Paraphrase 66–77.

5. Paraphrase 88–105.

*6. Try to account for the difficulty of these passages. Does it lie chiefly in the expression or style, as in Browning, or chiefly in the thought, as in Meredith's more cryptic poems? Does it seem right that a difficult thought should be clothed in a difficult style? At any rate, after making all allowance for the inheritance and environment of Miranda, we may feel that these speeches are somewhat too overpowering to address to a girl in her early 'teens. The crown and flower of wisdom is simplicity, as Prospero and his creator should have known.

7. Is there an adequate motive for the harshness of Prospero toward Ariel and Caliban? Is he fair to them?

8. Note and explain the differences between the punishments with which these two servants are threatened.

9. Are 387–395 pure soliloquy? Compare the first speech of *Richard III.*

10. Comment fully upon the effectiveness of the situation developed in 409 *ff.*

11. Are the thought and language of Miranda in all respects what you think appropriate to the circumstances?

12. Criticize the situation presented in l. 466 and stage direction. Show, if possible, that this is not a dramatic situation. This passage illustrates the fact that true drama cannot use and show the supernatural as the spring and efficient cause of human action.

13. What are the divisions of this scene?

14. What exposition do you find in the scene? Is it deftly introduced in all instances? Discuss especially the introduction of the long narrative of Prospero.

II, 1.

1. Do 1–184 seem in harmony with the spirit of the play? Why?

2. Differentiate the characters shown in these lines.

3. How does this passage prepare for the later conspiracy against Gonzalo and Alonso? Why is the conspiracy against Alonso introduced? What connection has it with the chief characters and events of the play?

4. Antonio is shown here treacherous, cowardly, and ready to repeat his former sin with less than his former motive, adding to his own guilt the guilt of tempting another. Compare the same man a few hours later, at the end of the play. Compare a similar eleventh-hour conversion in *As You Like It.*

II, 2.

1. Distinguish Trinculo and Stephano.

2. Explain Trinculo's change in attitude toward Caliban after l. 147.

III, 1.

1. Compare 1–15 with Ferdinand's earlier soliloquy.

2. What preparation has been made for Ferdinand's love at first sight? For Miranda's? Is this preparation adequate?

3. Are Miranda's words, actions, and thoughts in this scene what you would have imagined as appropriate?

4. Compare I, 2, 445, with 50–52. Comment.

III, 2.

1. How has Stephano won the worship of Caliban? What is the effect of this worship upon Stephano? Can you see any allegorical or symbolic meaning in this?

2. Upon what elements does the comic effect of 51–90 depend?

3. Are 144–152 suited to Caliban?

4. Why are Caliban's speeches in verse? Compare II, 2, 1–14.

III, 3.

1. Show that 21–34 intensify the stage illusion of reality.

2. How do 43–49a bear upon the circumstances under which they are spoken?

3. Paraphrase 75b–82.

4. Note the different effects of the enchantment upon the several persons present. What characterization do you find in this?

5. Do all those present hear the speech of Ariel? Why? Compare similar effects in *Macbeth* and *Hamlet*.

6. Comment upon the use of spectacle and of stage devices in this scene.

IV, 1.

1. Why has Prospero "punished" Ferdinand at all? See I, 2, 450–452a.

2. In what ways was the masque of spirits especially fitted for presentation at the court of James I on the occasion of his daughter's wedding?

3. How does this masque differ in its purpose and in its effect upon the spectators from that in III, 3?

4. What relation may 148–158 be supposed to have to the probability that *The Tempest* was Shakespeare's last play? Compare *As You Like It*, II, 7, 139b–140.

5. Memorize 148–158.

6. Is Prospero afraid of Caliban? How do you explain his vexation when he remembers the conspiracy?

*7. Are 230–234 consistent with the character of Caliban? Mention some of the difficulties involved in the delineation of this character. Does Browning solve these difficulties in his "Caliban upon Setebos" more successfully than Shakespeare?

8. Comment upon the humor in l. 250. Is there pathos in it as well? And satire?

9. Compare and contrast the punishment meted out to Caliban and his group with the punishment spoken of at the end of III, 3. Explain differences.

V, 1.

1. Does the sentence in 33–50 make complete sense? Why? Is the difficulty here in thought or in style?

2. What possibly autobiographical significance do you find in 33–57?

3. Were there graves on the island? See l. 48. Does it seem more than possible that the poet is thinking of himself here rather than of Prospero? In what sense do 48b–50a apply to the poet?

4. Paraphrase 141b–144a.

5. Comment upon the beauty of 182–184a. Is it because of her ignorance that Miranda speaks so? Does Prospero show the greatest possible wisdom in his reply? The world and mankind were very old to Shakespeare when he wrote this play, yet they were still "beauteous," "brave," and "new" to him. It is obvious that Prospero is not complete Shakespeare at all points. It is worth remembering that at the end of his last play the profoundest knower of the human heart wrote: "How beauteous mankind is!" The same mind that conceived Iago and Goneril felt, at the end, that the world is brave and new. For it must be clear that in the present passage the poet speaks more of his own thought in the fresh and dewy surprise of Miranda than in the wan and weary sapience of Prospero.

6. How was the chess game staged in Shakespeare's
   theater?
7. Are we asked to believe in a sudden conversion of the
   sinners in this play, as in *As You Like It*? How is
   this managed and why?
8. Is any good purpose served by the introduction of the
   seamen at the close of the play? What is lost by this?
9. Are all the actions closed and all legitimate questions
   answered by this last scene?

Hamlet - Indecision
Macbeth - Ambition
Richard III -   "
Brutus - Misguided Patriotism.